The
# Wiersbe
## BIBLE STUDY SERIES

Exhibiting

Real Faith

in the

Real World

**GENESIS 25—50**

David C Cook®

*transforming lives together*

THE WIERSBE BIBLE STUDY SERIES: GENESIS 25—50
Published by David C Cook
4050 Lee Vance View
Colorado Springs, CO 80918 U.S.A.

David C Cook Distribution Canada
55 Woodslee Avenue, Paris, Ontario, Canada N3L 3E5

David C Cook U.K., Kingsway Communications
Eastbourne, East Sussex BN23 6NT, England

The graphic circle C logo is a registered trademark of David C Cook.

All Scripture quotations in this study are taken from the Holy Bible, New
International Version®, NIV®. Copyright © 1973, 1984 by Biblica, Inc.™ Used by
permission of Zondervan. All rights reserved worldwide. www.zondervan.com.

In the *Be Authentic* excerpts, unless otherwise noted, all Scripture quotations
are taken from the King James Version of the Bible. (Public Domain.) Scripture
quotations marked NKJV are taken from are taken from the New King James Version®.
Copyright © 1982 by Thomas Nelson, Inc. Used by permission. All rights reserved;
and NIV are taken from the Holy Bible, New International Version®, NIV®.

All excerpts taken from *Be Authentic*, second edition, published by David C
Cook in 2010 © 1997 Warren W. Wiersbe, ISBN 978-1-4347-6630-4.

ISBN 978-0-7814-0636-9
eISBN 978-1-4347-0520-4

© 2012 Warren W. Wiersbe

The Team: Steve Parolini, Karen Lee-Thorp, Amy Konyndyk,
Nick Lee, Jack Campbell, Karen Athen
Series Cover Design: John Hamilton Design
Cover Photo: Veer

Printed in the United States of America
First Edition 2012

1 2 3 4 5 6 7 8 9 10

042512

# Contents

# Introduction to Genesis 25–50

## Imperfect Leaders

The main players in these chapters of Genesis—Isaac, Jacob, and Joseph—weren't perfect, but they were authentic in their relationships to themselves, their peers, and their God.

When they were frightened, they admitted it. When they were caught scheming, they suffered for it and learned from the pain. When they succeeded, they shared the blessing with others. When they prayed, they were desperate; and when they confessed sin, they were broken. In short, they were authentic, real, believable, down-to-earth people. Flawed? Of course! Occasionally bad examples? Certainly! Blessed of God? Abundantly.

## Authentic People

Why study these three authentic men? Because we live in a world of pseudo-saints and artificial heroes, many of whom are manufactured by the media and puffed by the promoters. The only thing some well-known Christians are known for is that they're well-known. Apart from that, there's nothing distinctive about them. They belong to the herd.

God is looking for authentic people who will dare to have firsthand spiritual experiences in life and not settle for the secondhand imitations that are promised if you listen to the right seminars, watch the right videos, and attend the right meetings.

"When people are free to do as they please," wrote Eric Hoffer, "they usually imitate each other." Authentic people struggle through life and let God make them the special individuals He planned for them to be.

*—Warren W. Wiersbe*

# How to Use This Study

This study is designed for both individual and small-group use. We've divided it into eight lessons—each references one or more chapters in Warren W. Wiersbe's commentary *Be Authentic* (second edition, David C Cook, 2010). While reading *Be Authentic* is not a prerequisite for going through this study, the additional insights and background Wiersbe offers can greatly enhance your study experience.

The **Getting Started** questions at the beginning of each lesson offer you an opportunity to record your first thoughts and reactions to the study text. This is an important step in the study process as those "first impressions" often include clues about what it is your heart is longing to discover.

The bulk of the study is found in the **Going Deeper** questions. These dive into the Bible text and, along with helpful excerpts from Wiersbe's commentary, help you examine not only the original context and meaning of the verses but also modern application.

**Looking Inward** narrows the focus down to your personal story. These intimate questions can be a bit uncomfortable at times, but don't shy away from honesty here. This is where you are asked to stand before the mirror of God's Word and look closely at what you see. It's the place to take a good look at yourself in light of the lesson and search for ways in which you can grow in faith.

**Going Forward** is the place where you can commit to paper those things you want or need to do in order to better live out the discoveries you made in the Looking Inward section. Don't skip or skim through this. Take the time to really consider what practical steps you might take to move closer to Christ. Then share your thoughts with a trusted friend who can act as an encourager and accountability partner.

Finally, there is a brief **Seeking Help** section to close the lesson. This is a reminder for you to invite God into your spiritual-growth process. If you choose to write out a prayer in this section, come back to it as you work through the lesson and continue to seek the Holy Spirit's guidance as you discover God's will for your life.

## Tips for Small Groups

A small group is a dynamic thing. One week it might seem like a group of close-knit friends. The next it might seem more like a group of uncomfortable strangers. A small-group leader's role is to read these subtle changes and adjust the tone of the discussion accordingly.

Small groups need to be safe places for people to talk openly. It is through shared wrestling with difficult life issues that some of the greatest personal growth is discovered. But in order for the group to feel safe, participants need to know it's okay *not* to share sometimes. Always invite honest disclosure, but never force someone to speak if he or she isn't comfortable doing so. (A savvy leader will follow up later with a group member who isn't comfortable sharing in a group setting to see if a one-on-one discussion is more appropriate.)

Have volunteers take turns reading excerpts from Scripture or from the commentary. The more each person is involved even in the mundane tasks, the more they'll feel comfortable opening up in more meaningful ways.

The leader should watch the clock and keep the discussion moving. Sometimes there may be more Going Deeper questions than your group can cover in your available time. If you've had a fruitful discussion, it's okay to move on without finishing everything. And if you think the group is getting bogged down on a question or has taken off on a tangent, you can simply say, "Let's go on to question 5." Be sure to save at least ten to fifteen minutes for the Going Forward questions.

Finally, soak your group meetings in prayer—before you begin, during as needed, and always at the end of your time together.

# Father and Son
## (GENESIS 25—26)

*Before you begin …*
- *Pray for the Holy Spirit to reveal truth and wisdom as you go through this lesson.*
- *Read Genesis 25—26. This lesson references chapter 1 in* Be Authentic. *It will be helpful for you to have your Bible and a copy of the commentary available as you work through this lesson.*

## Getting Started

### From the Commentary

Isaac was the son of a famous father (Abraham) and the father of a famous son (Jacob), and for those reasons he is sometimes considered a lightweight among the patriarchs. Compared to the exploits of Abraham and Jacob, Isaac's life does seem conventional and commonplace. Although he lived longer than either Abraham or Jacob, only six chapters are devoted to Isaac's life in the Genesis record, and only one verse in Hebrews 11 (v. 9).

Isaac was a quiet, meditative man (Gen. 24:63), who would rather pack up and leave than confront his enemies. During his long life, he didn't travel far from home. Abraham had made the long journey from Haran to Canaan, and had even visited Egypt, and Jacob went to Haran to get a wife, but Isaac spent his entire adult life moving around in the land of Canaan. If there had been an ancient Middle East equivalent to our contemporary "jet set," Isaac wouldn't have joined it.

—*Be Authentic*, page 17

1. How are the differences between Isaac and his father and son significant to the unfolding Genesis story? What does the fact that Isaac stayed close to home say about him? What does his story teach us about God?

*More to Consider: Respond to the following statement: Isaac wasn't a failure; he was just different. What made him different?*

2. Choose one verse or phrase from Genesis 25—26 that stands out to you. This could be something you're intrigued by, something that

makes you uncomfortable, something that puzzles you, something that resonates with you, or just something you want to examine further. Write that here.

# Going Deeper

*From the Commentary*

> Abraham recognized his other children by giving them gifts and sending them away, thereby making sure they couldn't supplant Isaac as the rightful heir. Along with his father's immense wealth (Gen. 13:2; 23:6), Isaac also inherited the covenant blessings that God had given Abraham and Sarah (12:1–3; 13:14–18; 15:1–6). Isaac had parents who believed God and, in spite of occasional mistakes, tried to please Him.

> Abraham's firstborn son, Ishmael (chap. 16), wasn't chosen to be the child of promise and the heir of the covenant blessings. God promised to bless Ishmael and make him a great nation, and He kept His promise (17:20–21; 25:12–16); "But my covenant will I establish with Isaac" (17:21; Rom. 9:6–13). Ishmael was on hand for his father's

funeral (Gen. 25:9), but he wasn't included in the reading of his father's will.

—*Be Authentic*, page 18

3. Review Genesis 25:1–18. In what ways does Ishmael picture or represent the unsaved person (1 Cor. 2:14)? How does Isaac portray someone who trusts Jesus (1 Peter 1:22–23)? What was the most important part of Isaac's legacy?

## From the Commentary

When Isaac was forty years old, God selected Rebekah to be his wife (Gen. 24; 25:20), and we have every reason to believe that they were both devoted to the Lord and to each other. The record indicates that Rebekah was the more aggressive of the two when it came to family matters, but perhaps that's just the kind of wife Isaac needed. Whatever mistakes Isaac may have made as a husband and father, this much is true: As a young man, he willingly put himself on the altar to obey his father and to please the Lord (chap. 22; Rom. 12:1–2).

Isaac and Rebekah waited twenty years for a family, but no children came.... Abraham and Sarah had to wait twenty-five years for Isaac to be born; Jacob had to labor fourteen years to obtain his two wives; and Joseph had to wait over twenty years before he was reconciled to his brothers. Our times are in His hands (Ps. 31:15), and His timing is never wrong.

—*Be Authentic*, pages 19–20

4. What kind of father was Isaac? Why did he and Rebekah wait so long for a family? What does the waiting reveal about God's sovereignty? Why might God choose to delay the gift of children to married couples?

## From Today's World

Genesis is littered with stories of husband and wife waiting on God to give them children and fulfill His promises. Throughout the Bible, God's timing with the arrival of children plays a critical role in His ongoing plan for salvation. In recent years, the scientific community has provided several (sometimes controversial) solutions to infertility. While there are many unsolved problems in the science of infertility, there are certainly more options available today than in the time of the patriarchs.

5. Is there room for God to work in a world shaped by science? How does the "waiting on God for children" truth still play out today? Does the medical community's attempt to end infertility leave God out of the equation? Where is God when science steps in?

## From the Commentary

One problem soon led to another, because Rebekah's pregnancy was a difficult one: The babies in her womb were struggling with each other. The Hebrew word means "to crush or oppress," suggesting that the fetal movements were not normal. Since Rebekah wondered if the Lord was trying to say something to her, she went to inquire. Isaac was fortunate to have a wife who not only knew how to pray, but who also wanted to understand God's will for herself and her children.

In salvation history, the conception and birth of children is a divinely ordained event that has significant consequences. This was true of the birth of Isaac (Gen. 18; 21), the twelve sons of Jacob (29:30—30:24), Moses (Ex. 1—2), Samuel (1 Sam. 1—2), David (Ruth 4:17–22), and our Lord Jesus Christ (Gal. 4:4–5). Conception, birth, and death are divine appointments, not human accidents, a part of God's wise and loving plan for His own people (Ps. 116:15; 139:13–16).

Imagine Rebekah's surprise when she learned that the two children would struggle with each other all their lives! Each child would produce a nation, and these two nations (Edom and Israel) would compete, but the younger would master the older. Just as God had chosen Isaac, the second-born, and not Ishmael, the firstborn, so He chose Jacob, the second-born, and not Esau, the firstborn. That the younger son should rule the elder was contrary to human tradition and logic, but the sovereign God made the choice (Rom. 9:10–12), and God never makes a mistake.

—*Be Authentic*, pages 20–21

6. Why is it significant that God chose the second-born child (in two instances) rather than the first to lead His people? In the context of a culture that revered the firstborn, what does this say about God? About God's people?

## From the Commentary

Esau probably means "hairy." He also had the nickname "Edom," which means "red," referring to his red hair and the red lentil soup Jacob sold him (Gen. 25:25, 30). The twin boys not only looked different but they also were different in personality. Esau was a robust outdoorsman, who was a successful hunter, while Jacob was a "home boy." You would think that Isaac would have favored Jacob, since both of them enjoyed domestic pursuits, but Jacob was Rebekah's favorite. Rebekah was a hands-on mother who knew what was going on in the home and could contrive ways to get what she thought was best.

It's unfortunate when homes are divided because parents and children put their own personal desires ahead of the will of God. Isaac enjoyed eating the tasty game that Esau brought home, a fact that would be important in later family history (chap. 27). Isaac, the quiet man, fulfilled his dreams in Esau, the courageous man, and apparently ignored the fact that his elder son was also a worldly man. Did Isaac know that Esau had forfeited his birthright? The record doesn't tell us. But he did know that God had chosen the younger son over the elder son.

A friend of mine kept a card under the glass on his office desk that read: "Faith is living without scheming." Jacob could have used that card. Before his birth, he had been divinely chosen to receive the birthright and the blessing; thus there was no need for him to scheme and take advantage of his brother. It's likely that Jacob had already seen plenty of evidence that Esau didn't care about spiritual things, an attitude that made Esau unfit to receive the blessing and accomplish God's will. Perhaps Jacob and his mother had even discussed the matter.

The name "Jacob" comes from a Hebrew word (*yaaqob*) that means "may God protect," but because it sounds like the words *aqeb* ("heel") and *aqab* ("watch from behind" or "overtake"), his name became a nickname: "he grasps the heel" or "he deceives." Before birth, Jacob and Esau had contended, and at birth, Jacob grasped his brother's heel. This latter action was interpreted to mean that Jacob would trip up his brother and take advantage of him. The prediction proved true.

—*Be Authentic*, pages 21–22

7. Did God allow apparent deception to determine the path of His plan? Explain. What does this say about the responsibility of those chosen by God? What choices did Rebekah, Jacob, and Esau each make during the selling of the birthright? How was each of them responsible for these choices and their consequences?

## From the Commentary

True faith is always tested, either by temptations within us or trials around us (James 1:1–18), because a faith that can't be tested can't be trusted. God tests us to bring out the best in us, but Satan tempts us to bring out the worst in us. In one form or another, each new generation must experience the same tests as previous generations, if only to discover that the enemy doesn't change and that human nature doesn't improve.

When Abraham arrived in Canaan, he found a famine in the land and faced his first serious test of faith (Gen. 12:10—13:4). His solution was to abandon the place God had chosen for him, the place of obedience, and to run to Egypt, thus establishing a bad example for his descendants who were prone to imitate him. The safest place in the world is in the will of God, for the will of God will never lead us where His grace can't provide for us. Unbelief asks, "*How* can I get out of this," while faith asks, "*What* can I get out of this?"

Isaac could flee from famine, but when he put himself into a situation that offered no escape, he had to turn to deception to protect himself. Abraham committed this same sin twice, once in Egypt (Gen. 12:14–20) and once in Philistia (chap. 20). Remember, faith is living without scheming, and telling lies seems to be one of humanity's favorite ways to escape responsibility.

Isaac was asked about the woman who was with him and, like his father Abraham before him, he said she was his sister. But when Abimelech saw Isaac caressing Rebekah, he knew she was his wife. Why did Isaac lie? Because he was afraid his pagan host would kill him in order to obtain his beautiful wife. His lie was evidence of his unbelief, for if he had claimed the covenant promise when he prayed for children (25:21), why couldn't he claim that same covenant promise to protect himself and his wife?

—*Be Authentic*, pages 23–24

8. Review Genesis 26:1–11. Note all the times Abraham is mentioned by name (or as "father"). Why is this significant to the story? Once again we see deception in one of God's chosen leaders. What does this say about the people God chooses to lead? What does it say about God's character? About God's covenant promise?

## From the Commentary

Isaac inherited flocks and herds from his father, who had lived a nomadic life, but now the wealthy heir settled down and became a farmer, remaining in Gerar "a long time" (Gen. 26:8).

Isaac and his neighbors had access to the same soil, and they depended on the same sunshine and rain, but Isaac's harvests were greater than theirs, and his flocks and herds multiplied more abundantly. The secret? God kept His promise and blessed Isaac in all that he did (vv. 3–5). God would give a similar blessing to Jacob years later (chap. 31).

God also blessed Isaac because of Abraham's life and faith (Gen. 26:5), just as He blesses us for the sake of Jesus Christ. We'll never know until we get to heaven how many of our blessings have been "dividends" from the spiritual investments made by godly friends and family who have gone before.

In spite of his material blessings, Isaac still suffered because of his lie, because the blessings he received brought burdens and battles to his life. Seeing his great wealth, the Philistines envied him and decided he was a threat to their safety. (A similar situation would occur when the Jews multiplied in Egypt. See Ex. 1:8ff.) "The blessing of the Lord makes one rich, and He adds no sorrow with it" (Prov. 10:22 NKJV). Had Isaac not lied about his wife, God would not have disciplined him but would have given him peace with his neighbors (Prov. 16:7). Because of his sin, however, Isaac's material blessings caused him trouble.

—*Be Authentic*, pages 25–26

9. Review Genesis 26:12–17. How could the Lord bless somebody who claimed to be a believer and yet had deliberately lied to his unbelieving neighbors? (See 2 Tim. 2:11–13.) What condition had God placed on His promise of blessing? What are some of the ways Isaac suffered, despite the blessing? What does this story teach us about God's promises? About how He responds to our disobedience?

*More to Consider: Read Genesis 26:34–35. In what ways was Isaac at peace with his neighbors but at war at home? How is this true with believers today?*

## From the Commentary

No matter where Isaac journeyed, the enemy followed him and confiscated his father's wells and also the new wells that Isaac's servants dug. To find a well of "springing water" (Gen. 26:19) was a special blessing, for it guaranteed fresh water at all times, but the Philistines took that well, too. The names of the new wells that Isaac's men dug reveal the problems that he had with his neighbors, for *Esek* means "contention," and *Sitnah* means "hatred." But *Rehoboth* means "enlargement" because Isaac finally found a place where he was left alone and had room enough for his camp and his flocks and herds.

Whenever Abraham had a problem with people, he boldly confronted them and got the matter settled, whether it was his nephew Lot (13:5–18), the invading kings (chap. 14), Hagar and Ishmael (21:9ff.), or the Philistines (vv. 22ff.). But Isaac was a retiring man who wanted to avoid confrontation. Since he was a pilgrim, he could move his camp and be a peacemaker.

Beersheba was a very special place for Isaac, because there his father had entered into a covenant with the Philistine leaders (21:22ff.). *Beersheba* means "the well of the oath." The Lord comes to us with His assuring Word just when we need encouragement (Acts 18:9–11; 23:11; 27:23–24; 2 Tim. 2:19). No matter who is against us, God is with us and for us (Gen. 28:15; 31:3; Rom. 8:31–39), and there's no need for us to be afraid. In response to God's gracious word of promise, Isaac built an altar and worshipped the Lord. He was ready to meet his adversaries.

—*Be Authentic*, pages 26–27

10. How did the different personalities of Isaac and his father play out in the way they dealt with adversity? What do their individual stories reveal about their relationship with God? About how God works?

## Looking Inward

Take a moment to reflect on all that you've explored thus far in this study of Genesis 25—26. Review your notes and answers and think about how each of these things matters in your life today.

*Tips for Small Groups: To get the most out of this section, form pairs or trios and have group members take turns answering these questions. Be honest and as open as you can in this discussion, but most of all, be encouraging and supportive of others. Be sensitive to those who are going through particularly difficult times and don't press for people to speak if they're uncomfortable doing so.*

11. Deception played a role in Isaac's story. What are some examples of deception you've seen recently in the church? Have you ever used deception to accomplish something you think God wanted? Explain.

12. Are you more like Abraham (dealing with difficulties head-on) or Isaac (preferring to avoid conflict)? How does this affect your relationship with other believers? With God? Is there only one godly way to deal with conflict? Explain.

13. God blessed Isaac and others because of His promise. What is God's promise to you? What are some of the blessings you've received from God because of that promise?

## Going Forward

14. Think of one or two things that you have learned that you'd like to work on in the coming week. Remember that this is all about quality, not quantity. It's better to work on one specific area of life and do it well than to work on many and do poorly (or to be so overwhelmed that you simply don't try).

Do you want to pay more attention to the way you deal with conflict? Be specific. Go back through Genesis 25—26 and put a star next to the phrase or verse that is most encouraging to you. Consider memorizing this verse.

*Real-Life Application Ideas: Consider your spiritual heritage for a moment. What role (if any) did your parents or other relatives play in your faith story? Record the significant events in your spiritual history, then consider how your story will influence the lives of those who come after you (whether your children, friends, peers, etc.). Then spend time in prayer, asking God to write for you a story that matters in the lives of others.*

## Seeking Help

15. Write a prayer below (or simply pray one in silence), inviting God to work on your mind and heart in those areas you've noted in the Going Forward section. Be honest about your desires and fears.

*Notes for Small Groups:*

- *Look for ways to put into practice the things you wrote in the Going Forward section. Talk with other group members about your ideas and commit to being accountable to one another.*

- *During the coming week, ask the Holy Spirit to continue to reveal truth to you from what you've read and studied.*

- *Before you start the next lesson, read Genesis 27—31. For more in-depth lesson preparation, read chapters 2 and 3, "A Masterpiece in Pieces" and "Disciplines and Decisions," in* Be Authentic.

# Decisions
## (GENESIS 27—31)

*Before you begin ...*
- *Pray for the Holy Spirit to reveal truth and wisdom as you go through this lesson.*
- *Read Genesis 27—31. This lesson references chapters 2 and 3 in* Be Authentic. *It will be helpful for you to have your Bible and a copy of the commentary available as you work through this lesson.*

## Getting Started

*From the Commentary*

Philosopher George Santayana called the human family "one of nature's masterpieces." If that's true, then many of these masterpieces have become nothing but pieces because they forgot the Master. Genesis 27 describes such a family.

Had I been alive during patriarchal times, I probably would have predicted great success for Isaac and Rebekah.

After all, Isaac was a dedicated man who had put himself on the altar in obedience to the Lord (Gen. 22; Rom. 12:1–2). He trusted God to choose his wife for him (Gen. 24), and the wife God sent, Isaac loved (v. 67). Both Isaac and Rebekah knew how to pray and seek the mind of the Lord for their home (25:19–23). What more could a married couple want?

—*Be Authentic*, page 33

1. In spite of all the advantages that Isaac and Rebekah had, their family self-destructed when Isaac became old. Why? What role did scheming play in the destruction? What role did selfishness play? What might have prevented such a family meltdown?

*More to Consider: A good beginning doesn't guarantee a good ending. That's one of the repeated lessons taught in Scripture, and it's tragically confirmed in the lives of people like Isaac, Lot, Gideon, Samson, King Saul, King Solomon, Demas, and a host of others. Why is this such a common story for biblical characters? Why do "bad endings" happen for people who start out so on fire for God? What are examples of this in today's church? How can it be prevented?*

2. Choose one verse or phrase from Genesis 27—31 that stands out to you. This could be something you're intrigued by, something that makes you uncomfortable, something that puzzles you, something that resonates with you, or just something you want to examine further. Write that here.

## Going Deeper

*From the Commentary*

Isaac was sure he was going to die, and yet his greatest desire was to enjoy a good meal at the hand of his favorite son and cook, Esau (Gen. 25:28). When Isaac's father, Abraham, prepared for death, his concern was to get a bride for his son and maintain the covenant promise. When King David came to the end of his life, he made arrangements for the building of the temple, and Paul's burden before his martyrdom was that Timothy be faithful to preach the Word and guard the faith.

Someone has well said, "The end of life reveals the ends of life." When sideshow promoter P. T. Barnum was dying, he asked, "What were today's receipts?" Napoleon cried out on his deathbed, "Army! Head of the army!" Naturalist Henry David Thoreau said only two words: "Moose … Indian."

—*Be Authentic*, page 34

3. In what ways does the end of life reveal the character of a person? What was Isaac's end-of-life request? What does this reveal about him? What message is there for us today in this ending?

## From the Commentary

Isaac was blind and apparently bedfast (Gen. 27:19, 31), a condition you would think would make him trust God and seek His help. Instead, Isaac rejected the way of faith and depended on his own senses: taste (vv. 4, 9, 25), touch

(v. 21), hearing (v. 22), and smell (v. 27). He took the scientific approach, and it failed him. "There are many plans in a man's heart, nevertheless, the LORD's counsel—that will stand" (Prov. 19:21 NKJV).

A character in Ernest Hemingway's novel *Death in the Afternoon* is probably expressing Hemingway's own convictions when he says, "I know only that what is moral is what you feel good after and what is immoral is what you feel bad after." Most people today would endorse that philosophy and make their decisions solely on the basis of how they feel, not what God says in His Word. "If it *feels* good, it *is* good!"

Isaac was a declining believer, living by the natural instead of the supernatural, and trusting his own senses instead of believing and obeying the Word of God. He was blind and bedfast and claimed to be dying, but he still had a good appetite. With a father like that leading the home, is it any wonder that the family fell apart?

—*Be Authentic*, page 35

4. Why would someone like Isaac stop trusting in the supernatural and trust the natural instead? What are some of the things that can strip away a person's long-held trust in God? What are some of the ways faith can remain strong even when trials and challenges come?

*From the Commentary*

> The obedience of faith was the secret of Abraham's life
> (Heb. 11:8), but the absence of obedient faith brought
> trouble to the home of Isaac and Rebekah.
>
> When Isaac sent for Esau to come to his tent, Rebekah
> noticed it and stayed close by to learn what was happen-
> ing. Later, when Esau revealed that he planned to kill
> his brother, Rebekah also heard that (Gen. 27:42), so
> she must have been adept at eavesdropping and keeping
> abreast of family affairs.
>
> However, it's tragic when a husband and wife, once so
> dedicated to the Lord and each other, have excommu-
> nicated each other and no longer discuss God's Word or
> pray together.
>
> Knowing that Jacob was chosen to receive the covenant
> blessing, Rebekah immediately took matters into her own
> hands to make sure her favorite son got what the Lord had
> promised him. Had she and Jacob talked with Isaac while
> Esau was out hunting, perhaps he would have seen the
> light and agreed with them. Instead, however, Rebekah
> chose to control Jacob and deceive her husband.
>
> —*Be Authentic*, page 36

5. What role did eavesdropping and scheming play in Rebekah's story?
Read James 3:13–18. In what ways is this passage a commentary on this

chapter in Isaac and Rebekah's life? What does the passage say for believers today?

## From the Commentary

Isaac's philosophy was "If it feels good, it is good," but Rebekah's philosophy was "The end justifies the means." She couldn't trust God to fulfill His plan; she had to help God out because it was for a good cause. But there's no place for deception in the life of the believer, for Satan is the deceiver (2 Cor. 11:3), but Jesus Christ is the truth (John 14:6). "Blessed is the man ... in whose spirit is no deceit" (Ps. 32:2 NIV).

In cooperating with the scheme, Jacob was only obeying his mother, but he could have refused and suggested that they just face the situation honestly and confront Isaac. But once Jacob donned Esau's clothes and took the savory meal in his hands, the die was cast and he had to play the part successfully. See how one lie led to another, for deception can be defended only by more deception. Jacob was weaving the tangled web.

Did Isaac ask for identification because he was hard of hearing? Probably not (Gen. 27:22); it's likely he was starting to get suspicious because he didn't expect Esau to return so quickly from the hunt (v. 20). Furthermore, the voice he heard didn't sound like the voice of Esau. That's when Jacob told his first lie: He claimed to be Esau.

He claimed to have obeyed his father's wishes (lie #2), and he called the goat's meat "my game" (lie #3). He even gave credit to the Lord for helping him find it so quickly (lie #4). He not only lied about himself, but he also lied about the Lord! To use the Lord to cover up sin is a step toward blasphemy.

Unwilling to trust his ears, Isaac felt Jacob's hands and mistook goatskin for human hair, and Jacob assured him again that he indeed was Esau (lie #5). How tragic it is to see a son so dishonor his father! After Isaac had eaten the meal, he asked Jacob to kiss him, and that kiss was the sixth lie, for it was hypocritical (Luke 22:48). How could Jacob claim to love his father when he was in the act of deceiving him? Since the smell of the garments finally convinced Isaac that Esau was there, the stage was now set for the giving of the blessing.

—*Be Authentic*, pages 37–38

6. Review Jacob's lies in Genesis 27:18–29. Do you think his lie about the Lord was worse than his lies about himself? Explain. Why didn't he go against his mother's wishes and do the honest thing in the first place? What

fears did he have about doing the honest thing? How does fear play into our decisions to lie or deceive?

## From the Commentary

Jacob had a close call and almost met Esau returning from the hunt. What lie would Jacob have told to explain why he was wearing Esau's clothes? It didn't take long for Isaac and Esau to discover the conspiracy, but each man responded differently.

One Hebrew scholar translates Genesis 27:33: "He trembled a trembling, a great, unto excess." Why was Isaac so agitated? Because he knew that the Lord had overruled his own selfish plan so that his favorite son did not receive the blessing. Isaac had lied to Abimelech in Gerar (chap. 26), and he had tried to lie to God by disobeying the Word (25:23), but now his own lies had caught up with him.

Esau, the man who had despised his birthright and married two pagan women, now wept and cried out for his father to bless him. It wasn't his fault, he told himself;

it was his crafty brother's fault. When in doubt, always blame somebody else.

—*Be Authentic*, pages 38–39

7. Compare Hebrews 12:16–17 with Genesis 27:30–40. Why are guilty people so quick to pass the blame to someone else, even when they know the truth will eventually come out? What are the key lessons in this story that we can apply to personal life? To community?

## From the Commentary

Jacob the "home boy" is now without a home and is starting on a five-hundred-mile trek to Haran. He was fleeing from an angry brother and facing an unknown future, and all he had to depend on was his father's blessing. From now on, the home boy would have to become a pilgrim and walk by faith. It was a three-day journey to Bethel, and those first three days of his adventure must have been very difficult. Would Esau follow him and try to kill him? Would he have enough food to keep him going (Gen. 32:10)? When he decided to spend the night at Bethel, he had no idea that God would meet him there; and from that night on, Bethel was a very special place to Jacob (35:1ff.).

Jacob slept on the earth with stones for his pillows (28:11, 18), a common practice in the Near East. The stone was probably more a protection than a pillow. As he slept, he had a dream in which he saw a ladder or stairway with angels going up and down between heaven and earth. Jacob discovered that he wasn't alone but that God was with him! The God of Abraham and Isaac was watching over him, and His angels were there to guard and serve him.

Jacob saw the Lord above him and then heard Him speak. The Lord didn't rebuke Jacob for participating in Rebekah's scheme; instead, He spoke words of promise and assurance to him. The same God who had cared for his father and grandfather pledged to care for him and to give him the very land on which he was lying. He would also multiply his descendants and fulfill the promise to bring blessing through them to all the world.

God would appear to Jacob at least five more times in the years ahead, but this first meeting was a significant one. He learned that God was interested in him and was at work in his life. From that night on, as long as he trusted the Lord and obeyed His will, he had nothing to fear.

—*Be Authentic*, pages 40–42

8. Review Genesis 28:10–22. What's most significant about Jacob's dream? Read the following passages: Deuteronomy 31:6–8; Joshua 1:5; 1 Samuel 12:22; 1 Chronicles 28:20; Matthew 28:20; Hebrews 13:5. What do these passages (and God's promise to Jacob) reveal about God's plan? About God's promises?

*More to Consider: Jacob's first response upon awakening from his dream was one of fear and surprise. How does Proverbs 1:7 speak to this response? What comfort might Psalm 90:1 offer someone in a similar situation?*

### From the Commentary

The Song of Solomon reminds us that the Jewish people never minimized the personal joys of marriage, but they also emphasized the responsibility of having children and building a God-fearing family. "Unless the LORD builds the house, they labor in vain who build it.… Behold, children are a heritage from the LORD, the fruit of the womb is a reward" (Ps. 127:1, 3 NKJV).

The Jews looked upon parenthood as a stewardship before God, and this was especially true in the case of Jacob, whose descendants would multiply "as the stars of the heaven, and as the sand which is upon the sea shore" (Gen. 22:17). God would honor him by making him the father of the twelve tribes of Israel, but the fact that four different women were involved in building his family would create for Jacob one problem after another.

—*Be Authentic*, page 51

9. Review Genesis 29:31—30:24. What does this passage reveal about the role of family in God's plan? Jacob had grown up in a divided and competitive home. How might this have contributed to the family he created? What does this reveal to us about the importance of parenting well?

## From the Commentary

The time had come for Jacob to move his large family to his own homeland and be on his own. He now had eleven sons and one daughter, and he had more than fulfilled his part of the bargain. He had earned the right to freedom. It was time to stop working for Laban and start building his own future security.

But crafty Laban wasn't about to lose his son-in-law, especially when he knew that Jacob's presence had brought to him the blessing of God (Gen. 30:27–30). Meanwhile, Laban wasn't interested in Jacob's God; he was interested only in the blessings he received because of Jacob's God. Laban surely knew of the promises God had made to Abraham and his descendants (12:3), and he wanted to get the most out of them.

This time, however, Jacob was prepared for his father-in-law, because the Lord had talked to Jacob in a dream and told him exactly what to do (31:1–13).

During the next six years, Jacob became a very wealthy man because of his faith and the blessing of the Lord. Now he was ready to strike out on his own, return to his own land and people, and fulfill whatever purposes God had planned for him. When he had arrived in Padan Aram twenty years before, all he had was his staff (32:10). But he had worked hard, suffered much, and trusted God. Now he had a large family and owned extensive flocks of healthy sheep and goats, as well as camels and donkeys and servants to care for all the animals.

—Be Authentic, pages 54–55

10. How did Laban take advantage of Jacob at each point in their relationship? How is this like or unlike the way some employers act toward their employees today? How did this mirror the way Jacob had treated his father and brother? What was God's answer to Jacob's potentially sticky employment situation (Gen. 31:1–3)? What unfinished business did Jacob have with his father and brother?

## Looking Inward

Take a moment to reflect on all that you've explored thus far in this study of Genesis 27—31. Review your notes and answers and think about how each of these things matters in your life today.

*Tips for Small Groups: To get the most out of this section, form pairs or trios and have group members take turns answering these questions. Be honest and as open as you can in this discussion, but most of all, be encouraging and supportive of others. Be sensitive to those who are going through particularly difficult times and don't press for people to speak if they're uncomfortable doing so.*

11. In what ways have you enjoyed a good beginning in your faith life? What good ending do you most hope for? What are some of the obstacles you may face in pursuit of that good ending?

12. Have you ever eavesdropped or schemed to get your way? If so, what prompted those choices? How did you feel afterward? How might you better have dealt with the situation? What role might faith play in that alternate solution?

13. Consider your family of origin. Do you see patterns of behavior in your own life that mirror those of your parents and other relatives? What are some of the positive things you've gained from your family of origin? What are some of the things you're hoping to change or overcome? How can trusting God help you with this?

## Going Forward

14. Think of one or two things that you have learned that you'd like to work on in the coming week. Remember that this is all about quality, not quantity. It's better to work on one specific area of life and do it well than to work on many and do poorly (or to be so overwhelmed that you simply don't try).

Do you want to learn how to live a life that has a good ending? Be specific. Go back through Genesis 27—31 and put a star next to the phrase or verse that is most encouraging to you. Consider memorizing this verse.

*Real-Life Application Ideas: Take a moment to consider the ways you've schemed or lied in the past to get something you want. Have you resolved all of those situations in a godly way? If there are any lingering issues that your poor decisions wrought, talk with a trusted counselor about how best to resolve those issues. Then take action to come clean before God and others in an appropriate, healing way.*

## Seeking Help

15. Write a prayer below (or simply pray one in silence), inviting God to work on your mind and heart in those areas you've noted in the Going Forward section. Be honest about your desires and fears.

*Notes for Small Groups:*

- *Look for ways to put into practice the things you wrote in the Going Forward section. Talk with other group members about your ideas and commit to being accountable to one another.*

- *During the coming week, ask the Holy Spirit to continue to reveal truth to you from what you've read and studied.*

- *Before you start the next lesson, read Genesis 32—34. For more in-depth lesson preparation, read chapter 4, "Catching Up with Yesterday," in* Be Authentic.

# Yesterday
## (GENESIS 32—34)

*Before you begin ...*
- *Pray for the Holy Spirit to reveal truth and wisdom as you go through this lesson.*
- *Read Genesis 32—34. This lesson references chapter 4 in* Be Authentic. *It will be helpful for you to have your Bible and a copy of the commentary available as you work through this lesson.*

## Getting Started

### From the Commentary

The slogan of the "Ingsoc Party" in George Orwell's novel *Nineteen Eighty-Four* was "Who controls the past controls the future: who controls the present controls the past."

That clever slogan may work for politicians who have the authority to rewrite history books, but nobody can change history itself. Two decades before, Jacob had fled from Esau to Laban, and now he was fleeing Laban only to be confronted by Esau! After twenty years, Jacob's past was catching up with him, and he was afraid. It's strange how we convince ourselves that we can escape the past and not reap what we've sown. We try to forget our sins, but our sins don't forget us. What Jacob did to his father and brother was forgiven by God, but neither time nor geography could change the consequences of those acts.

—*Be Authentic*, page 63

1. What are some of the conflicts Jacob faced during his life? What are some of the ways he flip-flopped in his faith? Respond to the following statement: A crisis doesn't make a man; it shows what a man is made of. How is this true in Jacob's story?

2. Choose one verse or phrase from Genesis 32—34 that stands out to you. This could be something you're intrigued by, something that makes you uncomfortable, something that puzzles you, something that resonates with you, or just something you want to examine further. Write that here.

# Going Deeper

*From the Commentary*

> "A brother offended is harder to win than a strong city"
> (Prov. 18:19 NKJV). Anticipating a difficult reunion with
> Esau, Jacob took the wise approach and sent messengers
> ahead to inform his brother that he was coming. But
> instead of committing the whole matter to the Lord, who
> had protected him from Laban, Jacob adopted a conde-
> scending attitude that wasn't befitting to the man God
> had chosen to carry on the Abrahamic covenant. Sending
> the messengers was a good idea, but calling Esau "my
> lord" and himself "your servant," and trying to impress
> Esau with his wealth, was only evidence that Jacob wasn't
> trusting God to care for him.
>
> —*Be Authentic*, page 64

3. Read Romans 8:31. How does this verse apply to Jacob's discovery of
the angels who had come to help him as he prepared to meet Esau? Why
does God use angels to remind His people of His role in their stories? What
does this tell us about Jacob? About God's methods for implementing His
grand plan?

*From the Commentary*

> As Jacob and his family, servants, flocks, and herds trav-
> eled slowly southwest toward Bethel, the messengers were
> moving rapidly to Mount Seir. By the time Jacob reached
> the Jabbok, a tributary of the Jordan, the messengers
> had returned with an ominous message: Esau and four
> hundred men were coming to meet Jacob. Expecting the
> worst, Jacob jumped to the conclusion that his brother
> had come to take vengeance on him and his family.
>
> —*Be Authentic,* page 65

4. How did Jacob's guilt affect his impending meeting with Esau? What
was he afraid of? How do Psalm 56:3 and Isaiah 12:2 speak to our fear?
How are they similar? How are they different? How would these messages
have helped Jacob?

*More to Consider: What are some of the things believers fear most
today? Read Psalm 112:7. How does this verse speak to that fear?*

## From Today's World

Jacob was skilled at hedging his bets. This isn't particularly a good skill to have, considering he was doing this in case God Himself didn't come through on His promises. In the corporate world, it's not unusual to have a backup or escape plan, especially where lots of money is concerned. We're also taught early on to backup our computer files and other important data in case something irreversible happens to them. Ours is a world of planning for the worst and hoping for the best. This is even true in some people's faith lives.

5. How does the "hedging your bets" philosophy make life better? In what ways can it limit us? How does it affect our faith? Is it easy to always trust God? What are the essential elements in trust? How can our trust in God help us grow our faith? Should people of faith ever hold anything back? Explain.

## From the Commentary

> Jacob's prayer is one of the great prayers recorded in Scripture, and yet it was prayed by a man whose faith was very weak. He was like the father of the demonized child who cried out, "Lord, I believe; help my unbelief!"

(Mark 9:24 NKJV). Every statement in this prayer indicates that Jacob had a profound knowledge of God's ways and God's character, and yet he was praying in desperation and not in confidence.

While we don't want to imitate Jacob's fear, unbelief, scheming, and his proneness to jump to conclusions, we would do well to pray the way he prayed.

—*Be Authentic*, pages 65, 67

6. Review Genesis 32:9–12. What were Jacob's arguments about why God should save him from Esau? In what ways did Jacob's desperation come through in his prayer? How are prayers of desperation different from confident prayers? What can we take away from Jacob's prayer that can help us when facing challenges or uncertain circumstances?

## From the Commentary

You would think that a prayer with that kind of solid theological content would have brought God's peace to Jacob's heart, but it didn't, and in his restlessness, he decided to act. "I will pacify him," he said (Gen. 32:20 NIV) and put together an expensive gift.

Sir Robert Walpole, England's first prime minister, said of Parliament, "All those men have their price." Many people of the world follow that philosophy ("Every man has his price"), the very philosophy Jacob was following as he put together his gift of 580 valuable animals. He divided them into separate herds and commanded the herdsmen to keep a space between each herd so that Esau couldn't help but be impressed with his brother's generosity.

Even more, each of the herdsmen was to make the same speech to Esau: "They belong to your servant Jacob. They are a gift sent to my lord Esau" (v. 18 NIV). With words like "your servant" and "my lord," Jacob was back to groveling again and ignoring the fact that God had made him lord over his relatives, including Esau (27:29). Jacob discreetly planned to follow behind the last drove, hoping that the combined impact of the gift would prepare Esau to forgive him and welcome him when they finally met.

—*Be Authentic*, pages 67–68

7. Review Genesis 32:13–21. Why was Jacob having such a hard time trusting God during this chapter of his story? How did he try to buy his comfort? Why do people tend to trust their own means when confronted with uncertainty? How does trusting God build a sense of surety in uncertain times?

*From the Commentary*

> It was dangerous to ford the river at night, but Jacob
> would rather hazard the crossing than risk losing his
> loved ones; so he moved his family to what he hoped
> was a safe place. Having forgotten about God's army, he
> wanted something between his family and his brother's
> army. Jacob devised his own two camps.
>
> —*Be Authentic*, page 68

8. Review Genesis 32:22–32. What did Jacob's wrestling encounter reveal
to him about God? About himself? Why does God often speak to us when
we're at the end of our resources?

*More to Consider: The Lord didn't ask "What is your name?" because He didn't know Jacob's name. Instead, He was asking if Jacob was going to continue his scheming or begin to trust God. Read the following passages: Genesis 17:4–5, 15; Numbers 13:16; John 1:40–42. What do these verses teach us about the importance of a "new name"? The new name God gave Jacob was "Israel," from a Hebrew word that means "to struggle." Why was this an appropriate new name for Jacob? (See also 2 Cor. 12:1–10.)*

## From the Commentary

Jacob had lifted up his eyes and seen the angels (Gen. 32:1–2), and he had even seen God face-to-face (v. 30), but when he saw Esau and his four hundred men, he seemed to lose everything he had gained in his struggle with himself and with the Lord. It's one thing to be blessed on the mountaintop with God and quite something else to carry that blessing down into the valley. Jacob failed himself, his family, and his God in several ways.

The "prince with God" stopped reigning and started scheming. Like too many of God's people today, he failed to live up to his new position in the Lord. By putting Rachel (his favorite wife) and Joseph (his favorite son) behind the other family members, he created a new problem in the home, and it's no wonder Joseph's brothers hated him in later years. You certainly knew where you stood in Jacob's household!

When Eastern peoples met in ancient days, they bowed often and exchanged traditional greetings ("Salaam" or "Shalom"), but there was more than tradition involved in the way Jacob and his family greeted Esau. Jacob was now a "prince with God," but he wasn't acting like it. "I have seen servants on horses, while princes walk on the ground like servants," said Solomon (Eccl. 10:7 NKJV), and Jacob was exhibit A of this tragedy. After all, the elder (Esau) was supposed to serve the younger (Gen. 27:29), so why should the younger brother bow?

—*Be Authentic*, page 71

9. Review Genesis 33:1–16. Why did Jacob continue to fall back to his own resources instead of trusting God? Where should Jacob have found his strength? How was his limp a reminder of God's nearness?

## From the Commentary

God's command was that Jacob return to Bethel (Gen. 31:13) and then to his home where Isaac still lived, which was Hebron (35:27). Instead, he tarried first at Succoth and then settled near Shechem. At Succoth, the pilgrim who was supposed to live in a tent (Heb. 11:9–16) built a house for himself and sheds for his flocks and herds. (The word *succoth* means "booths.") When he moved near Shechem, Jacob purchased a piece of property and became a resident alien in the land. He was settling down in the land.

It's obvious that Jacob wasn't in a hurry to obey God and return to Bethel. He built an altar and named it ("God, the God of Israel"). This indicates that he claimed his new name "Israel," but he certainly wasn't living up to all that his name implied. While he tarried in that part of the land, his daughter Dinah was raped and two of his sons became murderers. It was an expensive detour.

—*Be Authentic*, page 73

10. Once again Jacob was unable (or unwilling) to trust God's plan for his life. He made outward efforts, but his heart was divided. Read 1 Samuel 15:22. How does this verse speak to Jacob's situation? Did he think he was doing "enough" by building an altar? Why do believers try to second-guess what God asks of them? What does this reveal about their level of trust and maturity?

## Looking Inward

Take a moment to reflect on all that you've explored thus far in this study of Genesis 32—34. Review your notes and answers and think about how each of these things matters in your life today.

*Tips for Small Groups: To get the most out of this section, form pairs or trios and have group members take turns answering these questions. Be honest and as open as you can in this discussion, but most of all, be encouraging and supportive of others. Be sensitive to those who are going through particularly difficult times and don't press for people to speak if they're uncomfortable doing so.*

11. Have you ever held something back when serving or praying to God? What are some ways you've trusted yourself instead of God? Why did you do that? What would trust have looked like in those situations?

12. Which sort of prayers are you most comfortable with—prayers that come out of desperation or prayers that come from confidence in God? What have you learned from both kinds of prayer?

13. What do you do first when you come to the end of your resources in a situation? Where do you turn? What role does your faith play when you've run out of ideas? How can you grow your faith in these situations?

## Going Forward

14. Think of one or two things that you have learned that you'd like to work on in the coming week. Remember that this is all about quality, not quantity. It's better to work on one specific area of life and do it well than to work on many and do poorly (or to be so overwhelmed that you simply don't try).

Do you want to develop a deeper trust so you can stop holding things back with God? Be specific. Go back through Genesis 32—34 and put a star next to the phrase or verse that is most encouraging to you. Consider memorizing this verse.

*Real-Life Application Ideas: Uncertain times are often the best times to grow closer to God. Think about things in your life that are unsettled. This could be a family issue, a job situation, or even something to do with your church life. What is most unsettling about the situation? What are some ways you've already turned to God for help? What are some things you've tried to do on your own to resolve the situation? Consider talking with a pastor or small-group leader about how you can choose trust over self in this situation. Then do those things, being diligent to go to God in prayer throughout the duration of the situation.*

## Seeking Help

15. Write a prayer below (or simply pray one in silence), inviting God to work on your mind and heart in those areas you've noted in the Going Forward section. Be honest about your desires and fears.

*Notes for Small Groups:*

- *Look for ways to put into practice the things you wrote in the Going Forward section. Talk with other group members about your ideas and commit to being accountable to one another.*

- *During the coming week, ask the Holy Spirit to continue to reveal truth to you from what you've read and studied.*

- *Before you start the next lesson, read Genesis 35—37. For more in-depth lesson preparation, read chapters 5 and 6, "You Can Go Home Again" and "Enter the Hero," in* Be Authentic.

# Home and Hero
## (GENESIS 35—37)

*Before you begin …*
- *Pray for the Holy Spirit to reveal truth and wisdom as you go through this lesson.*
- *Read Genesis 35—37. This lesson references chapters 5 and 6 in* Be Authentic. *It will be helpful for you to have your Bible and a copy of the commentary available as you work through this lesson.*

## Getting Started

### From the Commentary

Moving from Genesis 34 to Genesis 35 is like going from a desert to a garden or from an emergency room to a wedding reception. The atmosphere in Genesis 35 is one of faith and obedience, and the emphasis is on cleansing and renewal. God is mentioned ten times in chapter 35, and He used His name *El Shaddai,* which means "God Almighty, the all-sufficient One." Best of all, in chapter 35 we see God's pilgrims making progress and arriving at the place of God's appointment.

However, Jacob's new step of faith didn't prevent him from experiencing new problems and trials.

—*Be Authentic*, page 79

1. Go through Genesis 35 and circle the mentions of God. What does this tell you about Jacob's ongoing story? What are some of the new trials Jacob faced during this renewal period? What are examples of trials believers face today in the midst of trusting God?

*More to Consider: The good news of the gospel is that we don't have to stay the way we are. No matter how many times we've failed the Lord, we can go home again if we truly repent and obey. This is true in Jacob's story (Gen. 35:1–15) and it also happened to other characters in the Bible. Review the following examples: Abraham (13:1–4), Isaac (26:17), David (2 Sam. 12), Jonah (Jonah 3:1–3), and Peter (John 21:15–19). What's similar in all these stories? What can we learn about "going home again" from these stories, as well as from Jacob's?*

2. Choose one verse or phrase from Genesis 35—37 that stands out to you. This could be something you're intrigued by, something that makes you uncomfortable, something that puzzles you, something that resonates with you, or just something you want to examine further. Write that here.

## Going Deeper

*From the Commentary*

For several years, Jacob had lingered thirty miles away from Bethel and had paid dearly for his disobedience. But now the Lord spoke to him and told him to move to Bethel and settle down there. Jacob already knew that Bethel was God's appointed place for him and his family (Gen. 31:13), but he had been slow to obey. "Remember therefore from where you have fallen; repent and do the first works" (Rev. 2:5 NKJV).

Jacob had built an altar on the property he had bought near Shechem and had called it "God, the God of Israel" (Gen. 33:20). But God wasn't pleased with this altar because He wanted him worshipping back at Bethel, "the house of God." The Lord reminded Jacob of his desperate situation over twenty years ago and how He had delivered him and blessed him. At Bethel, Jacob had made some vows to the Lord, and now it was time to fulfill them.

—*Be Authentic*, page 80

3. In what ways was Jacob's obedience to God incomplete? What does incomplete obedience look like in the church today? Why do believers choose to obey only in part? What do they hope to gain by doing this?

## From the Commentary

God had promised to bring Jacob safely back to Bethel (Gen. 28:15), and He kept His promise, as He always does (Josh. 21:45; 23:14; 1 Kings 8:56). Jacob kept his part of the agreement by building an altar and leading his household in worshipping the Lord. Once again, Jacob gave a new name to an old place. "Luz" he had renamed "Bethel, the house of God" (Gen. 28:19); and now "Bethel" he expanded to become "the God of Bethel." It wasn't the place that was important but the God of the place and what He had done for Jacob.

The Jewish people considered many places to be special because of what God had done for them there, places like Bethel, Mount Sinai, Jerusalem, the Jordan River, and Gilgal. Perhaps all of us have places that are especially meaningful to us because of spiritual experiences we had there, but a "holy site" must never take the place of the Holy God. To visit a special location and try to recapture old blessings is to live in the past. Let's ask God for new blessings and a new revelation of Himself!

—*Be Authentic*, page 82

4. Why did the Jewish people put so much importance on naming significant places in their history? What does the name of a place teach us about the people who named it? What are similar symbolic measures believers make today? How can they help remind us about our relationship with God?

## From the Commentary

Now we move from the voice of God to a baby's cry and a mother's last words.

When Jacob's beloved Rachel learned that she was pregnant, it must have given both of them great joy. She had borne Jacob only one son, Joseph ("adding"), and in naming him, she had expressed her desire for another son (Gen. 30:22–24). God answered her prayers and gave her a boy. Jacob now had twelve sons, the founders of the twelve tribes of Israel.

Rachel had said to Jacob, "Give me children, or else I die" (30:1). Now she would bear that second son, but in so doing would lay down her own life for the life of the child. We shouldn't interpret her death as a judgment from God either because of her rash statement or because she stole her father's idols. Life is a mosaic of lights and shadows, joys and sorrows, and the same baby that brought Rachel and her husband joy also brought tears.

*Ben-oni* means "son of my sorrow" or "son of my trouble," not a very favorable name for a man to carry through life, reminding him that his birth had helped cause his mother's death. Sorrow would overshadow his every birthday. But Jacob was always ready to rename something, so he called his new son *Benjamin*, which means "son of my right hand," that is, a son to be honored. The first king of Israel came from the tribe of Benjamin (1 Sam. 9), and the apostle Paul was also a Benjamite (Phil. 3:5).

More than twenty years before, Jacob had set up a pillar at Bethel to commemorate his meeting with God. Now he set up a pillar to memorialize his beloved wife Rachel. It was located "on the way to Ephrath," another name for

Bethlehem. (Ephrath means "fruitful," and "Bethlehem" means "house of bread.") Tradition places Rachel's tomb about a mile north of Bethlehem, on the road to Jerusalem, but Jeremiah said it was near Ramah, five miles north of Jerusalem (Jer. 31:15).

Were it not for the birth of Jesus in Bethlehem, the town would be remembered primarily for the death of Rachel. Because He came, we have "tidings of great joy" instead of tears of sorrow. Matthew connected Jeremiah's reference to Rachel with Herod's murder of the innocent children in Bethlehem (Matt. 2:18). The birth of Jesus brought joy (Benjamin) and also sorrow (Ben-oni).

—*Be Authentic*, pages 83–85

5. Review Genesis 35:16–20. What is significant about the way Jacob honored Rachel? What do the name changes in this story reveal about Jacob? About Jacob's current relationship with God? Why is this important?

## From the Commentary

The death of a dear wife is at least a normal human experience with no guilt attached, but what Reuben did was abnormal and stained with guilt and shame.

Reuben was Jacob's firstborn and therefore the oldest of his sons (Gen. 29:31–32); he was most likely in his twenties. The childhood episode with the mandrakes may or may not indicate anything about his nature (30:14–15). Bilhah was Rachel's maid and had borne Jacob two sons, Dan and Naphtali (vv. 1–8). Perhaps the recent death of Rachel left Bilhah desiring to be back with Jacob again, and this was Reuben's opportunity to act. Since the text doesn't indicate that Reuben raped his father's wife, we assume she cooperated in the deed.

But Reuben's sin involved much more than the satisfying of a lustful appetite. For a son to take a father's wife in this manner was a declaration that he was now the head of the family. When Abner took King Saul's concubine, Saul's son and heir Ishbosheth protested because it meant Abner was usurping the crown (2 Sam. 3:6–11). When David succeeded Saul as king, he was given Saul's wives as his own (2 Sam. 12:8). Rebellious Absalom declared himself ruler by taking his father's concubines (2 Sam. 16:20–23), and Adonijah's request to have Abishag as his wife was the same as challenging Solomon's rights to the throne (1 Kings 2:13–25).

It would appear, then, that Reuben's purpose was to take over the leadership of the family, which made his deed only that much more vile.

Those who teach that our dedication to the Lord automatically protects us from troubles and tears need to read this chapter carefully. Certainly God had forgiven Jacob, and certainly Jacob was walking with the Lord in faith and obedience. Nevertheless, he still had his share of trials. If we obey the Lord only for what we get out of it, and not because He is worthy of our love and obedience, then our hearts and motives are wrong. We become the kind of people Satan accused Job of being (Job 1:6—2:10).

—*Be Authentic*, pages 85–86

6. Why did Reuben act the way he did toward his father? What role might impatience have played? (See Luke 15:11–24.) Why didn't Jacob act right away in response to Reuben's sin? What was his eventual reaction? What does this story teach us about trials for those who follow God?

## From the Commentary

More than twenty years before, Isaac thought he was going to die (Gen. 27:1–4), but death didn't come until he was 180 years old. He lived the longest of all the patriarchs and yet less is recorded about his life than about his father, his sons, and his grandson Joseph.

We trust that Isaac and Jacob experienced a complete reconciliation and that the old patriarch died "full of years" as did his father (25:8). Esau came from Mount Seir to pay his respects to his father and to assist Isaac in burying him in the cave of Machpelah (49:29–32). Esau was a man of the world and not a child of the covenant, but he was still Isaac's son and Jacob's brother, and he had every right to be there. Death is a human experience that brings human pain to our hearts, and caring for the dead is a responsibility for all the family—believers and unbelievers.

—*Be Authentic*, page 86

7. Review Genesis 35:23—36:43. How did Isaac's death change Jacob's status? What does it mean to be the head of the family? How might the covenant blessing have affected the way he chose to live his life from then on?

*From the Commentary*

The author of a fourteenth-century preacher's manual wrote that envy was "the most precious daughter of the devil because it follows his footsteps by hindering good and promoting evil." The author might have added that Envy has a sister named Malice, and the two usually work together (Titus 3:3; 1 Peter 2:1). Envy causes inward pain when we see others succeed, and malice produces inward satisfaction when we see others fail. Envy and malice usually generate slander and unwarranted criticism, and when these two sins hide behind the veil of religious zeal and self-righteousness, the poison they produce is even more deadly.

British wit Max Beerbohm said, "People who insist on telling their dreams are among the terrors of the breakfast table." Should Joseph have told his dreams to the family, or was this just another evidence of his adolescent immaturity? The two dreams couldn't help but irritate the family and make things worse for him. After all, how could Joseph ever become a ruler, and why would his brothers bow down to him? The whole thing was preposterous. When Joseph reported the second dream, even his father became upset and rebuked him, but privately, Jacob pondered the dreams. After all, Jacob had received messages from God in dreams (Gen. 28:12ff.; 31:1–13), so perhaps it was the Lord who was speaking to Joseph.

*—Be Authentic*, page 95

8. Why is envy such a devious sin? What are ways it played into Joseph's story? Would it have been better for Joseph to keep his dreams from his family? Why or why not? How did God use Joseph's revelations to family members to further His plan? What does this reveal to us about God?

*More to Consider: Read Psalm 133:1. What are some ways Jacob's family didn't enjoy the blessings of unity? Why did the brothers hate Joseph so much? Why is family unity so important? Why is it so fragile? How does faith in God help build family unity?*

## From the Commentary

Envy is one of the works of the flesh that comes out of the sinful heart of man (Mark 7:22; Gal. 5:21). Because of their envy, Joseph's brothers sold him to the merchants. (See Matt. 27:18 and Mark 15:10 for a parallel to Christ's sufferings.) Their growing hatred was the equivalent of murder (Matt. 5:21–26), and though they didn't actually kill Joseph with their hands, some of them had done the deed many times in their hearts.

As we read Genesis 37:12–17, several questions come to mind. First, why were Jacob's sons pasturing their flocks fifty miles from home when there was surely good grassland available closer to Hebron? Possible answer: They didn't want anybody from the family spying on them. Second question: Why did they return to the dangerous area near Shechem when Jacob's family had such a bad reputation among the citizens there (34:30)? Suggested answer: The brothers were involved with the people of the land in ways they didn't want Jacob to know about.

—*Be Authentic*, page 97

9. Why did Jacob send Joseph out to visit his brothers alone and wearing the special garment that had aggravated them so much? How is this an example of God's providential hand? How did this accomplish God's plan?

## From the Commentary

Reuben was absent when his brothers sold Joseph, perhaps taking care of some problem with the sheep. Maybe he absented himself deliberately so they wouldn't suspect his hidden plan. When he visited the cistern, he was shocked to find that Joseph was gone. Thus he hurried back to the camp to find out what had happened. Certainly his attitude and actions made it clear to his brothers that his sympathies were with Joseph, for he tore his clothes like a man in mourning.

"He who covers his sins will not prosper" (Prov. 28:13 NKJV) is God's unchanging law, but people still think they can defy it and escape the consequences. Among Jacob's sons, one sin led to another as the men fabricated the evidence that would deceive their father into thinking that Joseph was dead, killed by a wild beast. Jacob would have no problem identifying the special robe, and he would have no way to test the blood. As tragic and treacherous as this deception was, Jacob was reaping what he himself had sown. Years before, he had killed a kid in order to deceive his father (Gen. 27:1–17), and now his own sons were following in his footsteps.

H. C. Leupold has translated 37:32, "And they sent the long-sleeved cloak and had it brought to their father." Unwilling to confront their father personally, the brothers sent a servant to Jacob to show him the "evidence" and tell him the lie that they had concocted. This was a brutal way to treat their father, but "the tender mercies of the wicked are cruel" (Prov. 12:10 NKJV).

Prone to jump to conclusions (Gen. 32:6–8), Jacob accepted the evidence, believed the story, and concluded that Joseph indeed was dead. He went into deep mourning, and twenty years later was still grieving over the death of Joseph (42:36). His family tried to comfort him but to no avail. His favorite son was dead, and Jacob thought he would carry his grief with him to the grave.

Years later, Jacob would lament, "All these things are against me" (v. 36), when actually all these things were working for him (Rom. 8:28).

—*Be Authentic,* pages 99–100

10. Review Genesis 37:29–36. Did God engineer or approve of the brothers' hatred of Joseph? Why or why not? How did God use this situation for His glory? How does this help us understand Romans 8:28? How is this like the way God used the ugliness of the cross in Jesus' story?

## Looking Inward

Take a moment to reflect on all that you've explored thus far in this study of Genesis 35—37. Review your notes and answers and think about how each of these things matters in your life today.

*Tips for Small Groups: To get the most out of this section, form pairs or trios and have group members take turns answering these questions. Be honest and as open as you can in this discussion, but most of all, be encouraging and supportive of others. Be sensitive to those who are going through particularly difficult times and don't press for people to speak if they're uncomfortable doing so.*

11. When have you been slow to obey God? What caused your hesitation? What was the result of your waiting? What was God trying to teach you in that situation? What did you learn?

12. In what ways have you obeyed God incompletely? Why do you struggle with complete obedience? What is the result of incomplete obedience? What steps can you take toward complete obedience?

13. God used an ugly situation to bring about His plan. What are some ways God has used difficult or ugly situations in your life for good?

## Going Forward

14. Think of one or two things that you have learned that you'd like to work on in the coming week. Remember that this is all about quality, not quantity. It's better to work on one specific area of life and do it well than to work on many and do poorly (or to be so overwhelmed that you simply don't try).

Do you want to become quicker to obey God? Be specific. Go back through Genesis 35—37 and put a star next to the phrase or verse that is most encouraging to you. Consider memorizing this verse.

*Real-Life Application Ideas: God repeatedly takes ugly situations and repurposes them for His glory. Consider the struggles you're currently facing. How might God use these situations for His good? What are ways you can open the door for God to act in those circumstances? Focus on seeing God's hand in all things this coming week—and look for opportunities to trust God despite the challenges you face, or perhaps because of them.*

## Seeking Help

15. Write a prayer below (or simply pray one in silence), inviting God to work on your mind and heart in those areas you've noted in the Going Forward section. Be honest about your desires and fears.

*Notes for Small Groups:*

- *Look for ways to put into practice the things you wrote in the Going Forward section. Talk with other group members about your ideas and commit to being accountable to one another.*

- *During the coming week, ask the Holy Spirit to continue to reveal truth to you from what you've read and studied.*

- *Before you start the next lesson, read Genesis 38—41. For more in-depth lesson preparation, read the interlude, "Judah and Tamar," and chapter 7, "The Lord Makes the Difference," in* Be Authentic.

# Difference Maker
## (GENESIS 38—41)

*Before you begin …*
- *Pray for the Holy Spirit to reveal truth and wisdom as you go through this lesson.*
- *Read Genesis 38—41. This lesson references chapter 7 in* Be Authentic. *It will be helpful for you to have your Bible and a copy of the commentary available as you work through this lesson.*

## Getting Started

### From the Commentary

The Egypt in which Joseph found himself was primarily a land of small villages inhabited by peasants who worked the land and raised grain and vegetables. Thanks to their system of irrigation, the annual flooding of the Nile River supplied ample water for both the crops and the cattle. There were some large cities such as On (Hieropolis), where Ra the sun god was, honored, and Memphis, devoted to Apis, the sacred bull, but most of the population lived in the small villages.

It was also a country shackled by religious superstition. The people recognized at least two thousand gods and goddesses, including Pharaoh himself, and the special emphasis was on preparing for the afterlife when the god Osiris would judge one's deeds. In a very real sense, Egypt was a land devoted to death as much as to life.

The Egyptians were great builders, and the rulers conscripted both slaves and their own citizens for vast building projects. While the common people lived in mud brick houses, the important structures were constructed of stone. (Some of the pyramids contain stones that weigh as much as fifteen tons.) The government was a large bureaucracy, with many officials at various levels and thousands of scribes to keep the records.

Egyptian priests and wise men studied the heavens and the earth, developed a solar year calendar of 365 1/4 days, and became well known for their medicines. They also perfected the art of embalming. The Egyptians had horses and chariots, and they knew the art of war.

—*Be Authentic*, pages 107–8

1. Why was the land in which Joseph found himself important to his ongoing faith story? How did his Jewish faith affect the way he was received? How did God use him to accomplish surprising things?

2. Choose one verse or phrase from Genesis 38—41 that stands out to you. This could be something you're intrigued by, something that makes you uncomfortable, something that puzzles you, something that resonates with you, or just something you want to examine further. Write that here.

## Going Deeper

*From the Commentary*

> When Joseph was at home in Hebron, his brothers considered him to be a troublemaker, but in Egypt, he was a source of blessing because God was with him. God promised Abraham that his descendants would bring blessing to other nations (Gen. 12:1–3), and Joseph fulfilled that promise in Egypt. Like the blessed man described in Psalm 1, everything he did prospered (Ps. 1:3; see also Josh. 1:8).

> Joseph is a good example of a believer who trusted God and made the best of his difficult circumstances. He never read what Jeremiah wrote to the exiles in Babylon (Jer. 29:7) or what Peter wrote to the scattered Christians in the Roman Empire (1 Peter 2:13–20), but he certainly put those instructions into practice. Joseph would rather have

been at home, but he made the best of his circumstances in Egypt, and God blessed him.

The blessing of the Lord was very evident to the people in Potiphar's household, and they knew that Joseph was the cause. "The LORD blessed the Egyptian's house for Joseph's sake" (Gen. 39:5), just as God had blessed Laban's house because of Jacob (30:27, 30). Potiphar gradually turned more and more responsibility over to Joseph until Joseph was actually managing the entire household, except for the food Potiphar ate.

Joseph was well liked by the people in Potiphar's house, and in pagan, idol-worshipping Egypt, Joseph was a testimony to the true and living God. He was an honest and faithful worker, and the people he lived and worked with got the message. God took note of Joseph's character and conduct and made him a blessing, and unknown to Joseph, God planned to fulfill the dreams He had sent him. "Do you see a man who excels in his work? He will stand before kings; he will not stand before unknown men" (Prov. 22:29 NKJV).

—*Be Authentic*, pages 108–9

3. Review Genesis 39:1–6. What are some of the ways Joseph lived out his faith while among pagans? What can today's believers glean from his example? In what ways was Joseph's service to others a blessing to himself?

*More to Consider: Read Matthew 25:21. How does this passage speak to the way Joseph's story played out? What are some of the ways God tests us before we can become leaders?*

## From the Commentary

Joseph had suffered in a pit because of the hatred of his brothers, but now he would face an even greater danger because of the lust of an evil woman. "For a harlot is a deep pit, and a seductress is a narrow well" (Prov. 23:27 NKJV).

Potiphar's wife treated Joseph in a humiliating way by inviting him into her bed. She may have reasoned, "After all, isn't he a Jew and a slave at that? And doesn't he work for my husband and therefore also work for me? Since my husband isn't here, I'm in charge, and Joseph is my employee. It's his job to take orders." She treated Joseph like a thing, not like a person; and when her advances were rejected, she turned against him.

No matter how much people talk about "love" and defend sex outside of marriage, the experience is wrong, cheap, and demeaning. Fornication and adultery change a pure river into a sewer and transform free people into slaves and then animals (5:15–23; 7:21–23). What begins as "sweetness" soon turns into poison (5:1–14). Joseph wasn't about to sacrifice either his purity or his integrity just to please his master's wife.

—*Be Authentic*, pages 109–10

4. What reasons did Joseph give Potiphar's wife about why he wouldn't sleep with her? How was he able to avoid giving in to that temptation? What role did his faith play in his response to her? What did this story reveal about Joseph's character?

## From Today's World

Turn on the TV or surf the Internet and you don't have to wait long before you come across news about a public figure's fall from grace. The moral failures of politicians, entertainers, and especially well-known men or women of faith is big news—the kind that makes the virtual front page and garners lots of comments from readers. Whether the claim is based on admission of guilt or mere rumor, the target is quickly judged guilty by many and defended with equally incomplete information by others. However, it's rarely (if ever) news if someone chooses to do the right thing—chooses the moral path instead of an opportunity to sin.

5. Why is our media so obsessed with people's moral failures? What does this say about our society? Why doesn't the media note integrity as readily as lack of integrity? Are there stories about the men and women who, like Joseph, chose to do the right thing? If so, how are these stories received by society at large?

*From the Commentary*

> Self-control is an important factor in building character
> and preparing us for leadership.... Joseph exercised self-
> control, but Samson used his body to gratify his own
> pleasures, and Joseph ended up ruling on a throne, while
> Samson ended his life buried in a pile of rubble (Judg.
> 16:23–31).
>
> For the second time in his life, Joseph lost a garment
> (Gen. 39:12; see also 37:23), but as the Puritan preacher
> said, "Joseph lost his coat but he kept his character." Since
> Potiphar was involved in the Egyptian judicial system, we
> wonder why he didn't try to put Joseph on trial or even
> execute him. Of course, God was in control, working out
> His wonderful plan for Joseph, Egypt, Joseph's family,
> and the world.
>
> —*Be Authentic*, pages 110–11

6. Read Proverbs 25:28. How does this verse apply to Joseph's choices?
Why is integrity so important for a leader? How do people become men and
women of integrity? What role does God play in our pursuit of integrity?

## From the Commentary

"They bruised his feet with shackles, his neck was put in irons," said the psalmist (Ps. 105:18 NIV), but these experiences aren't mentioned in Genesis. Perhaps Joseph was bound for a short time, but it wasn't long before the prison warden released him and put him in charge of the other prisoners. Like Potiphar before him, the warden turned everything over to Joseph and watched the work prosper in his hands.

God permitted Joseph to be treated unjustly and put in prison to help build his character and prepare him for the tasks that lay ahead. The prison would be a school where Joseph would learn to wait on the Lord until it was His time to vindicate him and fulfill his dreams. Joseph had time to think and pray and to ponder the meaning of the two dreams God had sent him.

—*Be Authentic*, page 111

7. Respond to the phrase *God's delays are not God's denials.* How was this true in Joseph's story? How did Joseph's imprisonment build his character? What does this teach us about one of the ways God helps us build character? What are other ways God builds character in His people?

*More to Consider: Dreams played a very important part in the life of leaders in Egypt, and the ability to interpret dreams was a highly respected skill. Why do you think dreams were so important to the Egyptian leaders? How did God prepare Joseph for his role as an interpreter of dreams?*

## From the Commentary

As far as the Genesis record is concerned, there are only two instances of Joseph displaying unbelief; the first is in 40:14–15, 23. (The second is in 48:8–20 when Joseph tried to tell Jacob how to bless the two grandsons.) Knowing that the cupbearer would be released and have access to Pharaoh, Joseph asked him to speak a good word for him and get him out of the prison. Joseph was putting his trust in what a man could do instead of depending on what God could do. He was getting impatient instead of waiting for God's time.

Joseph didn't mention his brothers or accuse them of evil. He only said he was "stolen" (kidnapped) from home and therefore was not a slave but a free man who deserved better treatment. His use of the word "dungeon" in 40:15 (see also 41:14) doesn't necessarily mean that he and the other prisoners were in a terribly wretched place. They were confined in the jail for the king's prisoners (39:20), which is called "the house of the captain of the guard" (40:3), so it was certainly not a dungeon. It may well have been house arrest. Joseph was speaking just as you and I would speak when we want people to sympathize with our plight: "This place is the pits!"

—*Be Authentic*, page 113

8. Though he'd been standing strong and trusting God for most of his time in Egypt, Joseph succumbed to the temptation to trust in people instead, if only for a moment. What led to this unbelief? What are the clues that we're starting to trust people over God? Where can we turn when we're starting to lose faith in a God who appears absent?

## From the Commentary

Two years have passed, and Joseph is still working in the prison house, waiting for something to happen. But when things started to happen, events began to move quickly, for God's time had come to activate His plans for Joseph. If any chapter in Genesis reveals the sovereignty of God, it's chapter 41.

God caused Pharaoh to have two dreams the same night, dreams that perplexed him and that his magicians (soothsayers) couldn't interpret. Note the repetition of the word "behold" in verses 1–7, emphasizing the vividness of the dreams and the rapidity of the sequence. Unlike King Nebuchadnezzar, he didn't forget his dreams (Dan. 2) but shared them with his wise men. These men may have been gifted at understanding dreams, but God so worked that they were unable to interpret them.

Since the time had come for Joseph to be delivered from prison and given a throne, God prodded the cupbearer's memory so he could recall what had happened to him in prison. His report about Joseph's abilities to understand dreams was exactly what Pharaoh wanted to hear. The fact that Joseph was called a Hebrew (Gen. 41:12) didn't bother Pharaoh, because Semitic people were accepted in Egypt and even promoted to hold important positions in the government. Certainly Pharaoh would recall the dramatic events involving the baker and the cupbearer.

Since the Egyptian people didn't wear beards in that day, as did the Hebrews, Joseph had to shave himself, change his clothes, and prepare to meet Pharaoh. For the third time in thirteen years, he gave up his garment, but this time he would gain the garment of a ruler.

We commend Joseph for his humility and desire to honor the true and living God (v. 16; see also 40:8; Dan. 2:27–28). He listened to Pharaoh describe his two dreams and then gave him the interpretation. It was a serious matter, for God had shown the ruler of Egypt what He planned to do for the next fourteen years, and Pharaoh was conscious of this fact. Now that he knew God's plan, Pharaoh was obligated to do what God wanted him to do.

—*Be Authentic*, pages 114–15

9. Review Genesis 41:1–45. Why do you think Joseph went beyond giving an interpretation to making suggestions to Pharaoh? How did Pharaoh respond to Joseph's demeanor, his skill at interpreting dreams, and his wisdom? How was this another example of God preparing and using His people to move history according to His plan?

## From the Commentary

Over a period of thirteen years, God enabled Joseph to accomplish some wonderful things. He brought blessing to Potiphar's house and to the people in the prison. He overcame temptation, and because of that, he endured false accusation and great injustice. Joseph was a man of faith who expected God to work, and he was ready and obedient when the call came. But there was one more achievement that in some ways was greatest of all: He was enabled by God's grace to wipe out the pains and bad memories of the past and make a new beginning.

Certainly a man who could interpret the dreams of others could interpret his own dreams. Joseph must have concluded that the famine would bring his brothers to Egypt, and that meant he would have to confront them with their sins against him and their father. He wanted his own heart to be clean and right before God so that he could be a blessing to them just as he'd been a blessing wherever God had placed him.

The name *Manasseh* means "forgetting." Joseph didn't forget his family or the events that occurred, but he did forget the pain and suffering that they caused. He realized that God meant it for good (50:20).

—*Be Authentic*, page 116

10. In what ways was Joseph a man who expected God to work? Why is this important to his story? To our stories today? How was the way Joseph looked at his past an example of forgiveness? How did it prepare him for the events to come?

## Looking Inward

Take a moment to reflect on all that you've explored thus far in this study of Genesis 38—41. Review your notes and answers and think about how each of these things matters in your life today.

*Tips for Small Groups: To get the most out of this section, form pairs or trios and have group members take turns answering these questions. Be honest and as open as you can in this discussion, but most of all, be encouraging and supportive of others. Be sensitive to those who are going through particularly difficult times and don't press for people to speak if they're uncomfortable doing so.*

11. Think back to a time when you were being severely tempted or tested. How did you respond in that situation? If you gave in to temptation, what led to that choice? How did that make you feel? How did you recover from your choice? If you beat the temptation, what helped you to do that? Why is it sometimes difficult to trust God when you're being tested?

12. How would you define *integrity*? What are some clues that you are a person of integrity? What are the things that challenge your integrity?

How do you stay grounded with integrity? What role does your faith play in integrity?

13. Joseph was good at trusting God, but there were a couple of times when he began to doubt God's presence. Describe a time when you began to doubt God would help you in your life. What led to that doubt? How did you work through it? If you trusted people instead of God, what were the results? How might the outcome have been different if you'd trusted God?

## Going Forward

14. Think of one or two things that you have learned that you'd like to work on in the coming week. Remember that this is all about quality, not quantity. It's better to work on one specific area of life and do it well than to work on many and do poorly (or to be so overwhelmed that you simply don't try).

Do you want to work on being able to trust God more when you feel tempted? Be specific. Go back through Genesis 38—41 and put a star next to the phrase or verse that is most encouraging to you. Consider memorizing this verse.

*Real-Life Application Ideas: Do an informal survey on the topic "What does it mean to have integrity?" Ask coworkers, friends, family members, and others for their opinions. Then compare what they say to what the Bible says about the subject. Take a close look at your own behaviors, choices, and habits to see how you compare to those definitions. Thank God for all the ways He's helped you to live a life of integrity, then ask him for help with those areas where you struggle to be a person of integrity.*

## Seeking Help

15. Write a prayer below (or simply pray one in silence), inviting God to work on your mind and heart in those areas you've noted in the Going Forward section. Be honest about your desires and fears.

*Notes for Small Groups:*

- *Look for ways to put into practice the things you wrote in the Going Forward section. Talk with other group members about your ideas and commit to being accountable to one another.*

- *During the coming week, ask the Holy Spirit to continue to reveal truth to you from what you've read and studied.*

- *Before you start the next lesson, read Genesis 42—45. For more in-depth lesson preparation, read chapters 8 and 9, "When Dreams Come True" and "Truth and Consequences," in* Be Authentic.

# Truth and Consequences

## (GENESIS 42—45)

*Before you begin …*
- *Pray for the Holy Spirit to reveal truth and wisdom as you go through this lesson.*
- *Read Genesis 42—45. This lesson references chapters 8 and 9 in* Be Authentic. *It will be helpful for you to have your Bible and a copy of the commentary available as you work through this lesson.*

## Getting Started

### From the Commentary

After the promised seven years of plenty, the years of famine came upon the Middle Eastern world, but thanks to Joseph, there was abundant grain in Egypt. God had sent Joseph ahead (Gen. 45:5; Ps. 105:17) to preserve his family so that one day the nation of Israel could give the world Jesus Christ, the "bread of life" (John 6:48).

These events took place during the first two years of the seven-year famine (Gen. 45:6). It was a time when Joseph's brothers had to experience several tests that were designed by God to bring them to repentance.

Jacob had a large family (46:26) and many servants, and as the famine continued, it became more and more difficult to feed them. Certainly the brothers knew what their father knew, that there was grain in Egypt, but they didn't talk about it. Jacob noticed their strange attitude and asked, "Why do you keep staring at each other?" Why, indeed, did the brothers hesitate to talk about the problem or even offer to go to Egypt to purchase food?

For one thing, the trip to Egypt was long (250–300 miles) and dangerous, and a round trip could consume six weeks' time. Even after arriving in Egypt, the men couldn't be certain of a friendly reception. As foreigners from Canaan, they would be very vulnerable and could even be arrested and enslaved. If that happened to Jacob's sons, who would care for their families and their aged father?

—*Be Authentic*, page 122

1. Review Genesis 42:1–24. What role might the brothers' guilty consciences have played in their hesitation to go to Egypt to collect grain during the famine? How does guilt affect our ability to act?

*More to Consider: God often uses dramatic circumstances to accomplish His purposes. In addition to the famine described in Genesis, consider the following: God used a kidnapping (2 Kings 5:2–3), a royal beauty contest (Est. 2), a sudden death (Ezek. 24:15–27), a dream (Dan. 2), a plague (Joel 1), and even a government census (Luke 2:1–7). Why does God sometimes choose such dramatic actions? (See Ps. 115:3.)*

2. Choose one verse or phrase from Genesis 42—45 that stands out to you. This could be something you're intrigued by, something that makes you uncomfortable, something that puzzles you, something that resonates with you, or just something you want to examine further. Write that here.

## Going Deeper

*From the Commentary*

> Joseph put his brothers in confinement for three days, just to teach them what it was like to be prisoners and to give them time to think. The KJV translates the Hebrew word as "prison" (or "ward") in Genesis 42:17, but "in custody" would be closer to the original. The word translated "prison" in Genesis 39—40, describing Joseph's experiences, means a prison and not just being under guard or

house arrest. Joseph suffered as a prisoner in a real prison, while his brothers were only confined under guard. But it taught them a lesson. When they were released three days later, the ten men were beginning to sense that God was dealing with them because of their sins (42:21).

When I think of the way Joseph behaved toward his brothers, the verse that comes to mind is Romans 11:22: "Behold therefore the goodness and severity of God" ("Consider therefore the kindness and sternness of God," NIV). Joseph was certainly kind to his brothers in spite of the severity of his speech and some of his actions, and what he did was for their good.

—*Be Authentic*, pages 124, 126

3. What was Joseph's motivation for the way he treated his brothers? What was his goal? What does this reveal to us about the way God sometimes treats us?

## From the Commentary

When the nine brothers prepared to leave Egypt, Joseph graciously provided food for their journey. It wasn't easy for them to leave Simeon behind, but they were sure they'd return for more grain and be able to bring Benjamin with them. It seemed that the clouds were starting to lift, but they didn't realize the tensions that were yet to come in their family in the days ahead.

At Joseph's command, his steward replaced the brothers' money in their sacks, but later the steward said he had received their silver and he gave credit to the Lord (Gen. 43:23). Either the steward was lying, which is doubtful, or Joseph paid for the grain himself so that he could care for his father and the relatives he hadn't seen in over twenty years. The money in the sacks was also part of his plan to test his brothers and prepare them for their next trip to Egypt.

But there are some problems relating to the discovery of the money. When one brother found the silver in his sack (42:27–28), all the men must have searched through their sacks and found the rest of the silver. At least that's the story they told Joseph's steward when they arrived in Egypt on their second visit (43:21). But if that's what happened, why did the brothers act surprised and frightened when they opened their sacks on arriving home (42:35)?

To say that their account to the steward was merely a "condensed report" of what had happened is to accuse them of having very poor memories. They specifically stated that it was at "the lodging place" ("the inn," KJV), and not at home, that they discovered the money in the sacks. We assume that this statement is correct because they had no reason to lie to Joseph's steward, the one man whose help they desperately needed. And why lie when they were returning all the money?

What are the possible solutions? Perhaps the steward put some of the money in the provision sacks and some in the grain sacks. The money in the provision sacks was found when they camped for the night, but the rest of the money wasn't discovered until they emptied the other sacks at home. But the writer clearly stated that each man found all his money at the first stopping place (43:21; "the exact weight," NIV), which means that the nine brothers had done a quick search immediately and found all the silver.

If that's true, then perhaps the brothers replaced the money in the sacks with the intention of deceiving their father by acting surprised when the money was discovered at home. But 42:35 is written as though their surprise and fear were genuine responses to finding the money. And why deceive their father about the money? They hadn't stolen it, and they could take it back on their next trip. Anyway, Jacob didn't seem worried about it; his only comment was "Perhaps it was a mistake" (43:12 NIV).

Whatever the explanation, the experience put fear and perplexity into the hearts of the brothers. "What is this that God has done to us?" they asked (42:28 NKJV). They knew that they were innocent concerning the money, but could they convince the Egyptians?

—*Be Authentic*, pages 126–27

4. Review Genesis 42:25—43:15. Why was the discovery of money a source of tension for the brothers? How might their lives have been endangered by the money (see 43:18)? Why is it valuable to try to understand this piece of the story? What insights can we gain from learning about Joseph's intent and the brothers' response to the money?

## From the Commentary

It was all too much for Jacob. "It is always me that you bereave," he cried (Gen. 42:36), thus hinting that he suspected his sons were behind Joseph's mysterious disappearance. "All these things are against me!" was a valid statement from a human point of view, but from God's perspective, everything that was happening was working for Jacob's good and not for his harm (Rom. 8:28).

It's sad to see Jacob again expressing his special love for Joseph and Benjamin, something that must have hurt the other sons. Hadn't the ten boys made the difficult trip to Egypt to help preserve the family? Was it their fault that the Egyptian officer asked too many personal questions, called them spies, and took Simeon as hostage? Were they responsible for the return of the money? Jacob could have been more understanding, but he was still grieving the loss of Joseph (Gen. 37:35); and the loss of Simeon and the possible loss of Benjamin were more than he could bear.

Considering that Reuben was out of favor with his father (35:22), Reuben should have kept quiet, but perhaps he felt obligated to act like a leader since he was Jacob's first-born son. His suggestion was ridiculous. What right did he have to offer his sons' lives as compensation for the loss of Benjamin? Did he discuss this idea with his wife and sons? Furthermore, how would the death of two innocent boys offset the loss of one of Jacob's two favorite sons? Was Reuben offering to sacrifice one son for Joseph and one for Benjamin? How would this make matters better in the home?

Jacob would have nothing to do with Reuben's suggestion or with any suggestion that threatened Benjamin's safety. The statement "he is left alone" (42:38) means "Benjamin alone is left of Rachel's two sons." It was another selfish statement from Jacob that made the other sons feel they were second-class members of the family. Benjamin must be protected even if the whole family starves! A crisis doesn't make a man; it shows what a man is made of.

Jacob was revealing his true affections, just as he had done when he had met Esau (33:2).

—*Be Authentic*, pages 128–29

5. What are some of the family dynamics at play in this part of the story? How might Jacob's apparent favoritism have affected the way the brothers acted? Why would Reuben offer such a dramatic solution to the crisis? What does this say about Reuben and his relationship with his father? What does this entire scene teach us about the role family relationships plays in our growing faith lives?

## From the Commentary

There's a difference between surrendering to God's loving providence and bowing to blind fate, and Jacob's statements show where he stood. "If it must be so.... If I be bereaved of my children, I am bereaved" (Gen. 43:11, 14). This kind of response certainly doesn't sound like the Jacob of Bethel who claimed the promises of God and had angels caring for him! Nor is it the Jacob who led his family back to Bethel for a new beginning with the Lord.

His feelings of grief and despair had almost extinguished his faith.

Always the controller, Jacob told his sons exactly what to do. Of course, there had to be a present for the Egyptian ruler who could release Simeon (32:13ff.); and they had to take twice the amount of money so they could return the money they found in their sacks as well as purchase more food. It's interesting that Jacob said, "Take your brother also" (43:13 NIV), and not, "Take also my son." Was he emphasizing their personal responsibility to take care of their own flesh and blood?

He sent them off with his blessing (v. 14), asking that *El Shaddai* (God Almighty, the All-Sufficient One) change the heart of "the man" so he would show mercy by releasing Simeon and not hurting Benjamin. But his final statement didn't give evidence of much faith or hope: "If I be bereaved of my children [Joseph, Benjamin, and Simeon], I am bereaved." Perhaps he wanted those pathetic words to echo in his sons' minds as they journeyed to Egypt.

—*Be Authentic*, page 130

6. Why was Jacob such a negative thinker when it came to the situation with his sons? Where was his faith during this time? In what ways was he planning for the worst? Why wouldn't he choose hope (as he had in previous seasons of life) over distrust and despair?

*From the Commentary*

The nine brothers had enough to think about on their trip without pondering their father's chronic grief. In fact, they faced three difficult problems for which they had no answers: (1) Explaining to the officials why they had the money, (2) effecting Simeon's release from confinement, and (3) protecting Benjamin. But by the time they were heading back home, they thought all these problems had been solved.

This was a time of transition as the brothers moved from fear to peace, for punishment because of the money was no longer an issue; from bondage to freedom, for Simeon had been released; and from anxiety to joy, for Benjamin was not in danger. So Joseph's brothers ate and drank as if there were no famine in the land, and they rejoiced at the generosity of the ruler at the head table.

—*Be Authentic*, pages 130–32

7. Review Genesis 43:16–34. Respond to the following statement as it applies to the actions of Joseph's brothers: It's one thing to be relieved and quite something else to be forgiven and reconciled. Why is it perilous to experience false joy? What are the dangers of believing God is blessing us just because life happens to be good?

## From the Commentary

> Joseph had one more stratagem in his wise plan for bring-
> ing his brothers to repentance, and this one involved his
> own beloved full brother, Benjamin. Once Jacob's sons
> had faced their sins and repented, Joseph could reveal
> who he was, and they could be reconciled.
>
> When the eleven brothers left Joseph's house, they had
> every reason to be joyful (Gen. 43:34). They hadn't been
> arrested for stealing the grain money, Simeon had been
> released, Benjamin was safely traveling with them, and
> they were going home at last. They had also been honored
> guests at a wonderful feast, and the generous ruler had
> sent them on their way with their sacks full of grain. It
> was indeed a happy day.
>
> But their joy was only a mirage.
>
> —*Be Authentic*, page 138

8. In what ways was the brothers' joy based on lies? What are other examples of ways people live a false joy or peace? What is the only true source of peace? (See Isa. 32:17.)

*More to Consider: It was Judah who suggested the brothers sell Joseph (Gen. 37:26–27), and it was Judah who unwittingly committed incest with his daughter-in-law (chap. 38). Knowing these facts about Judah, why do you think he was the new spokesman for the family (44:14)? What does this reveal to us about the power of God to change people?*

## From the Commentary

> Since this was an official meeting, other Egyptian officers were present, but now that he was about to settle a long-standing family matter, Joseph wanted his brothers all to himself. His interpreter, and perhaps other officials present, would understand their conversation in Hebrew, and everybody would be able to witness the brothers' tears and expressions of love. It was time for family privacy.
>
> —*Be Authentic*, page 142

9. Review Genesis 45:1–15. Why did Joseph want privacy to discuss this family matter? What does this tell us about Joseph's character? What can we learn from this decision that applies to us today?

## From the Commentary

The Egyptians whom Joseph had asked to leave the room probably lingered close to the door so they could be the first to find out what was going on and report it to Pharaoh. When they heard Joseph and his brothers weeping and understood why, they carried the news to Pharaoh who rejoiced that Joseph's brothers were now with him. After all, Joseph was the savior of the nation and a "father" to Pharaoh (Gen. 45:8), and the ruler of Egypt wanted to give a royal welcome to Joseph's family.

Joseph had already told his brothers to relocate in Egypt. So it's likely that he and Pharaoh had previously discussed this idea and that Pharaoh had approved. Pharaoh's words not only verified what Joseph had promised, but also they promised even more. He promised them "the fat of the land" to enjoy and wagons for carrying their families and whatever goods they wanted to bring with them to Egypt. Because of Joseph, Jacob and his family had the great ruler of Egypt working for them and providing what they needed!

The brothers had taken Joseph's robe from him when they sold him to the merchants (37:23), but he gave each of them new clothes to wear. In Scripture, a change of clothes is often the sign of a new beginning (35:1–7; 41:14), and this was certainly a new beginning for Jacob's eleven sons.

Joseph's brothers had sold him for twenty pieces of silver, but Joseph gave Benjamin fifteen times that amount.

He also provided the men with extra food and ten extra animals to carry the food and to draw the carts for their return to Egypt with their families. It would take a great deal of food to feed Jacob and sixty-five members of his family as they traveled to Egypt.

Jacob was happy to see his sons safely home again, especially Benjamin, about whom he had been particularly concerned. But Jacob wasn't prepared for the incredible report that (1) Joseph was alive; (2) he was the second ruler of Egypt; (3) he wanted the whole family to move to Egypt; and (4) he would care for all of them. How much good news can an old man handle in one day?

"Jacob's heart fainted" (45:26) literally means his heart "grew cold" or "grew numb." He almost had a heart attack! The news was too good to believe, but he couldn't deny the presence of the carts that Joseph had sent and the extra animals to carry the burdens and draw the carts. His spirit revived as he contemplated seeing Joseph and having his united family around him until he died. He was 130 years old when he went to Egypt (47:9) and he died at 147, which means he had seventeen years in which to enjoy the family, especially Joseph and the two grandchildren he had never seen before (v. 28).

—*Be Authentic*, pages 145–47

10. Review Genesis 45:16–28. How did God reveal His goodness to Jacob's family in this passage? What do we learn about God in Joseph's response to

his brothers? In Pharaoh's kindness toward all of Jacob's family? What are the key takeaways from this story?

## Looking Inward

Take a moment to reflect on all that you've explored thus far in this study of Genesis 42—45. Review your notes and answers and think about how each of these things matters in your life today.

*Tips for Small Groups: To get the most out of this section, form pairs or trios and have group members take turns answering these questions. Be honest and as open as you can in this discussion, but most of all, be encouraging and supportive of others. Be sensitive to those who are going through particularly difficult times and don't press for people to speak if they're uncomfortable doing so.*

11. When have you felt despair and helplessness? What led to those feelings? What do you think God was doing during that time? How can you learn to trust God rather than assume the worst? Why is that often difficult? What are the benefits of learning to trust in those situations?

12. Joseph forgave his brothers for their truly terrible abuse of him, and he dealt with them in a shrewd way that drew them toward repentance. When have you faced a decision about whether to forgive someone? How easy has it been for you to let go of bitterness toward that person? How do you go about deciding how to deal with such people?

13. Jacob eventually went from grieving to rejoicing when the news that Joseph was alive reached him. What are some examples in your life when you've been surprised by good news that overwhelms the sadness or grieving you've been feeling? What are some of the ways God has surprised you with great news?

## Going Forward

14. Think of one or two things that you have learned that you'd like to work on in the coming week. Remember that this is all about quality, not

quantity. It's better to work on one specific area of life and do it well than to work on many and do poorly (or to be so overwhelmed that you simply don't try).

Do you want to learn how to be as forgiving as Joseph? Be specific. Go back through Genesis 42—45 and put a star next to the phrase or verse that is most encouraging to you. Consider memorizing this verse.

*Real-Life Application Ideas: Think about the people in your community who are currently experiencing difficult seasons in life. Perhaps someone is struggling financially because of a job loss. Or maybe someone is struggling with family issues—a prodigal son or daughter, a family member caught in addiction. Consider those who are grieving the loss of a loved one or the broken bonds of friendship. First, pray for the person, asking God for wisdom in how you might offer comfort. Then take practical action to offer that comfort (when appropriate) to the person in need. Think of Jacob and all that he suffered and how a kind word, a listening ear, might have helped him to work through the uncertainty.*

## Seeking Help

15. Write a prayer below (or simply pray one in silence), inviting God to work on your mind and heart in those areas you've noted in the Going Forward section. Be honest about your desires and fears.

*Notes for Small Groups:*

- *Look for ways to put into practice the things you wrote in the Going Forward section. Talk with other group members about your ideas and commit to being accountable to one another.*

- *During the coming week, ask the Holy Spirit to continue to reveal truth to you from what you've read and studied.*

- *Before you start the next lesson, read Genesis 46—49. For more in-depth lesson preparation, read chapters 10 and 11, "Grandfather Knows Best" and "The Family with a Future," in* Be Authentic.

#  Family Matters
## (GENESIS 46—49)

*Before you begin ...*
- *Pray for the Holy Spirit to reveal truth and wisdom as you go through this lesson.*
- *Read Genesis 46—49. This lesson references chapters 10 and 11 in* Be Authentic. *It will be helpful for you to have your Bible and a copy of the commentary available as you work through this lesson.*

## Getting Started

*From the Commentary*

A Jewish proverb says, "For the ignorant, old age is as winter, but for the learned, it is a harvest." Jacob was now 130 years old, and during those years, he had learned many important lessons about God, himself, and other people, especially his sons. Some of those lessons in the school of life had been difficult to learn, and Jacob hadn't always passed every test successfully. But now, thanks to God's goodness and Joseph's faithfulness, Jacob would reap a rich harvest in Egypt during the next seventeen years. His closing years wouldn't bring winter with its cold and storms. Jacob's sunset years would be as the autumn, with the warm golden sunshine of peace and the bounties of God's gracious harvest.

—*Be Authentic*, page 151

1. What does Jacob's final chapter—lived out in Egypt and relative luxury—reveal about God's promises? What does it teach us about waiting on God? Does this mean all who trust God will have happy, fruitful final years? Why or why not?

2. Choose one verse or phrase from Genesis 46—49 that stands out to you. This could be something you're intrigued by, something that makes you uncomfortable, something that puzzles you, something that resonates with you, or just something you want to examine further. Write that here.

# Going Deeper

*From the Commentary*

Jacob and his family left Hebron (Gen. 37:14) and traveled for about a week until they came to Beersheba, the southernmost town in Canaan (Josh. 15:21, 28). Beersheba was a very special place to Jacob, for there Abraham had dug a well (Gen. 21:30) and there Abraham lived after offering Isaac on Mount Moriah (22:19). Isaac had also lived at Beersheba (26:23, 32–33), and it was from the home in Beersheba that Jacob left for Laban's house to find a wife. At Beersheba, God had appeared to Hagar (21:17) and to Isaac (26:23–24), and now He would appear to Jacob.

Since Jacob was about to leave his own land and go into a strange country, he paused to build an altar and worship the Lord…. I recall seeing an entire family come to the front of the church at the close of a worship service and kneel to pray. Since the father was in the armed forces and was being transferred to another base, the whole family joined him in committing themselves to the Lord for this new venture.

But why should Jacob worry about going to Egypt? Didn't his son Joseph instruct him to come? Wasn't it the wisest thing to do in light of the continued famine in the land? Perhaps Jacob was fearful because he remembered that his grandfather Abraham had gotten into serious trouble by going to Egypt (12:10ff.). And when Jacob's father, Isaac, started toward Egypt, the Lord stopped him

(26:1–2). Egypt could be a dangerous place for one of God's pilgrims.

But the Lord came to Jacob at night and assured him that it was safe for him and his family to relocate.

—*Be Authentic*, page 152

3. Why did Jacob build altars in times of transition or change? Why is it important to ask for God's special help and blessing when we're about to enter a new phase in life? How did Jacob do that?

*More to Consider: It must have encouraged Jacob to see how God had multiplied his descendants, protected them, provided for them, and kept them together for the move to Egypt. The record lists first the sons, daughter, and grandsons of Leah (Gen. 46:8–15), followed by the families of Zilpah (vv. 16–18), Rachel (vv. 19–22), and Bilhah (vv. 23–25), a total of seventy people. Why is it significant that the Bible records so many details of Jacob's family? What confidence does this list give us about God's promises? How does this record offer evidence that God keeps His promises? (See Gen. 15:5; 22:17; 26:4; 32:12.)*

## From the Commentary

The eleven brothers had already been reunited with Joseph, but now Jacob would meet him after a separation of twenty-two years. That Jacob chose Judah to be their guide indicates that he trusted his son, which suggests that the men had told their father everything and were in his good graces again. Now Jacob could see the hand of God in all that had happened. In spite of his past failures, Judah now proved himself faithful, and his descendants were eventually named the royal tribe (Gen. 49:8–12).

The land of Goshen was located in the northeast part of the Nile delta, an area of about nine hundred square miles, very fertile and excellent for grazing cattle. It was there that Joseph and his father met each other, Joseph waiting in his royal chariot and Jacob riding in one of the wagons Pharaoh had provided. For the fifth time, we find Joseph weeping, although there's no specific statement that Jacob wept. Perhaps Jacob was so overcome with joy and thanksgiving to God at seeing Joseph again that he was unable to shed tears.

—*Be Authentic*, page 154

4. Read Luke 2:29–30. How is this passage similar to Genesis 46:30? Why was Jacob preoccupied with sorrow and death rather than with the joys of spending his latter years with his family? How had Joseph's dreams come true in this chapter of his story?

## From the Commentary

Joseph was careful to brief his family on what it meant to be a shepherd in Egypt. The fact that Jacob's sons had brought their flocks and herds along indicated clearly that they were planning to stay in Egypt and continue their occupation. Knowing that the Egyptians were prejudiced against shepherds, Joseph's emphasis was on the herds of cattle and not the flocks of sheep. However, they didn't lie about their occupation but were honest and aboveboard in all their dealings with Pharaoh.

We don't know which five of his brothers Joseph selected to represent the family or why they were chosen. A keen student of human nature and a discerning man, Joseph knew which of his brothers could best meet Pharaoh and make a good appearance. But Pharaoh kept his promises and gave them the best of the land for their families and their flocks and herds, and he requested that they care for his herds as well. This was quite a promotion for the eleven sons of Jacob. One day they were ordinary resident aliens, and the next day they were Pharaoh's official herdsmen! Joseph had been kind to Pharaoh, and now Pharaoh showed kindness to Joseph's family.

—*Be Authentic*, page 155

5. Review Genesis 46:31—47:6. Why did Pharaoh show such kindness to Joseph's family? What does this tell us about the importance of being a person of integrity no matter where we end up?

## From the Commentary

Jacob had enjoyed Joseph for seventeen years in Hebron (Gen. 37:2), and now he would enjoy Joseph and his sons for seventeen years in Egypt (47:28). It was tragic that the sins of his sons had robbed their father of twenty-two years of Joseph's life, but even in this sacrifice, God had beautifully worked out His plan and cared lovingly for His people.

Since Jacob had rejected Reuben, Joseph was now performing the duties of the firstborn son, including the burial of the father. Jacob knew that his days were numbered, and he wanted to be sure that he would be buried in the Promised Land and not in Egypt. Someone might argue that Jacob was making a mistake, because the Egyptians were experts at interring bodies, but that wasn't the issue. Jacob was one of God's pilgrims, and he wanted to be buried with his family in the land that would one day be home for his descendants (49:29–32; 23:1ff.).

—*Be Authentic*, page 157

6. In what ways was Jacob's desire to be buried in the Promised Land a witness to others about his faith? What does Jacob's last witness say about him? How can such a witness impact the lives of others?

## From the Commentary

Genesis 49 is usually titled "Jacob Blesses His Sons," but Jacob used the word "bless" only with reference to Joseph (vv. 25–26). Three times in verse 28 we're told that Jacob's words were "a blessing" upon the sons, and in a prophetic sense, they certainly were, for Jacob announced what the Lord had in store for them in the future. But Jacob's "blessing" was much more than that.

For one thing, Jacob's words were a revelation of human character and conduct as well as of divine purposes. Three of the sons learned that their past conduct had cost them their future inheritance (vv. 3–7), for we always reap what we sow. But something else was true: Jacob's prophetic words must have given great encouragement to his descendants during their difficult time of suffering in Egypt, as well as during their unhappy years wandering in the wilderness. Jacob assured each tribe of a future place in the Promised Land, and that meant a great deal to them.

But even more, you find in Jacob's "last witness and testimony" a beautiful revelation of the gracious Lord who had cared for His servant for so many years. There's also a revelation of the Messiah, who had been promised to Jacob's people. In these words of Jacob, you meet Shiloh (v. 10), Salvation (*Yeshua*, v. 18), the Mighty One, the Shepherd, the Stone (v. 24), and the Almighty (v. 25), all of which point to our Savior, Jesus Christ.

As he addressed them, Jacob followed the birth order of the sons, beginning with Leah's six sons and closing with Rachel's two sons, Joseph and Benjamin.

—*Be Authentic*, pages 163–64

7. Describe the "blessings" each of Jacob's sons received. What do these blessings reveal about the consequences of our behavior? About Jacob's understanding of God? About God Himself?

*From the Commentary*

God gave Jacob six sons by Leah, the wife he didn't want (Gen. 29:31–35; 30:14–21). She was distinguished by being the mother of Levi, who founded the priestly tribe, and Judah, the father of the royal tribe.

—*Be Authentic*, page 164

8. What blessings did God give each of Leah's sons? What happened to the blessings given to Reuben, Simeon, and Levi? What does this reveal about godly character? About the importance of that character to God?

*From the Commentary*

> Jacob didn't hesitate to make it known that Rachel was
> his favorite wife and that her two sons were his favorite
> children. This kind of favoritism caused a great deal of
> trouble in the family, and yet God overruled it to accom-
> plish His own purposes. Jacob said more about Joseph
> than about any of the other sons, but he didn't have much
> to say about Benjamin.
>
> —*Be Authentic*, page 170

9. Review Genesis 49:22–27. How did favoritism cause problems in Jacob's
family? How was this revealed in the blessings? How did God overcome
the favoritism to accomplish His divine purpose?

*From the Commentary*

> The statements that Jacob made to each of his sons would
> be remembered by them and repeated to the members of
> their family for years to come. As time passed, they would
> see new and deeper meanings in these pronouncements,

and they would treasure the assurances Jacob had given them from the Lord.

But the old man's last statements were about himself, not about his sons, for he wanted them to guarantee that they would bury him in the cave of Machpelah where the bodies of five members of his family were now resting. Abraham had purchased the cave as a burial place for Sarah (Gen. 23), but over the years Isaac, Rebekah, and Leah had been buried there, and now Jacob would join them. He had already spoken about this matter to Joseph (47:27–31), so he knew his requests would be followed, but he wanted all his sons to know they had the responsibility of obeying his last commands and showing respect for their father.

*—Be Authentic,* pages 172–73

10. Why was it important to Jacob that his sons respect his wishes concerning his burial? Even though Jacob would not be able to double-check that they'd done what he asked, he wanted assurance that they understood his desire. How is this a model of what it means to trust?

## Looking Inward

Take a moment to reflect on all that you've explored thus far in this study of Genesis 46—49. Review your notes and answers and think about how each of these things matters in your life today.

*Tips for Small Groups: To get the most out of this section, form pairs or trios and have group members take turns answering these questions. Be honest and as open as you can in this discussion, but most of all, be encouraging and supportive of others. Be sensitive to those who are going through particularly difficult times and don't press for people to speak if they're uncomfortable doing so.*

11. How do you mark seasons of change in your life? What signposts do you trust when facing change? What markers do you place to honor the changes God presents to you?

12. What do you want your lasting witness to say to others? If you knew you were about to die, how would you prepare that witness so others would know of your faith? What can you do every day to ensure your final days are a witness to God?

13. What are some ways favoritism has caused problems in your family or circle of friends? How do you go about solving problems caused by favoritism? What is the biblical answer to playing favorites? How can learning to trust help overcome the temptation to play favorites?

## Going Forward

14. Think of one or two things that you have learned that you'd like to work on in the coming week. Remember that this is all about quality, not quantity. It's better to work on one specific area of life and do it well than to work on many and do poorly (or to be so overwhelmed that you simply don't try).

Do you want to learn how to avoid playing favorites? Be specific. Go back through Genesis 46—49 and put a star next to the phrase or verse that is most encouraging to you. Consider memorizing this verse.

*Real-Life Application Ideas: The blessings given to Jacob's family members are evidence of their father's love for them and indicators of how well they lived out their lives. Think about the people you would like to bless for their contribution to your life. This could include family members, friends, coworkers, teachers—anyone who has been a blessing to you. Then do something symbolic to show how much you appreciate those people. Write a letter, give a gift, offer your time— whatever fits the person. Don't ask for anything in return—just show the people how much you value what they've done to help you grow your faith.*

## Seeking Help

15. Write a prayer below (or simply pray one in silence), inviting God to work on your mind and heart in those areas you've noted in the Going Forward section. Be honest about your desires and fears.

*Notes for Small Groups:*

- *Look for ways to put into practice the things you wrote in the Going Forward section. Talk with other group members about your ideas and commit to being accountable to one another.*

- *During the coming week, ask the Holy Spirit to continue to reveal truth to you from what you've read and studied.*

- *Before you start the next lesson, read Genesis 50. For more in-depth lesson preparation, read chapters 12 and 13, "Three Coffins" and "Be Authentic," in* Be Authentic.

# Endings
## (GENESIS 50)

*Before you begin ...*
- *Pray for the Holy Spirit to reveal truth and wisdom as you go through this lesson.*
- *Read Genesis 50. This lesson references chapters 12 and 13 in* Be Authentic. *It will be helpful for you to have your Bible and a copy of the commentary available as you work through this lesson.*

## Getting Started

### From the Commentary

I once asked a friend what the death rate was in his city, and he replied quietly, "One apiece." That's the ratio everywhere.

Death isn't an accident, it's an appointment (Heb. 9:27). "It's not that I'm afraid to die," wrote Woody Allen. "I just don't want to be there when it happens." But he'll be there, and you and I will be there when it happens to us. Nobody has yet figured out how to peek into God's appointment book and erase the date.

Genesis 50 records three burials, two of them literal and one figurative, and all of them important.

—*Be Authentic*, page 177

1. Why does the Bible record so many burials? What does this reveal to us about the people who were buried? What does it teach us about God?

2. Choose one verse or phrase from Genesis 50 that stands out to you. This could be something you're intrigued by, something that makes you uncomfortable, something that puzzles you, something that resonates with you, or just something you want to examine further. Write that here.

# Going Deeper

*From the Commentary*

The scene was a solemn one. Jacob had nothing more to say. So he drew himself into the bed, lay down, and went to sleep with his sons standing around him and his God waiting for him. He left behind the nucleus of a great nation and the testimony of what a great God can do with an imperfect man who sought to live by faith. He exchanged his pilgrim tent for a home in the heavenly city (Heb. 11:13–16).

"Old men must die," wrote Alfred, Lord Tennyson, "or the world would grow moldy, would only breed the past again."

Perhaps. But when old people die, those who love them feel the loss deeply. The longer you have someone in your life that you really love, the deeper the roots go into your heart and the more wrenching is the experience of having those roots pulled up. Yes, grief is a normal part of life, and believers don't grieve "as others who have no hope" (1 Thess. 4:13 NKJV). But death is still an enemy, and when he slinks in and robs us of someone dear, we feel the pain for a long time.

*—Be Authentic*, pages 177–78

3. Review Genesis 50:1–14. Verse 1 says, "Joseph threw himself upon his father and wept over him." What does this reveal about Joseph's feelings

for his father? Why was it important for Scripture to record Joseph's tears here? What does this tell us about the value God places on expressing emotions?

*More to Consider: Anglican poet and pastor John Keble said tears are "the best gift of God to suffering man." Read Psalm 30:5. What does this verse teach us about the role of tears in grief? How is the Bible's teaching on grief applicable to us today?*

## From the Commentary

Joseph had his father's body properly prepared for burial, a skill the Egyptians had mastered. To do the work, he chose the physicians and not the official embalmers, probably to avoid the pagan religious rituals that accompanied the Egyptian embalming process. Jacob was a believer in the true and living God and didn't need the help of the gods of the Egyptians. Centuries later, Moses would call down plagues on the land and show how weak the Egyptian gods and goddesses really were.

Pharaoh commanded the Egyptians to observe an official mourning period for Jacob. After all, Jacob was the father of the second ruler in the land. This kind of recognition was usually reserved for important people like Pharaoh himself or members of his family. The forty days of the embalming period and the seventy days of the official mourning were probably concurrent.

Why did Joseph use the court officials to take his message to Pharaoh instead of speaking to him personally? Perhaps Joseph was considered defiled because of his father's death, or there may have been an Egyptian tradition that prevented mourners from approaching the king (Est. 4:2). As a "father" to Pharaoh, Joseph had to get permission to leave the country, and he also had to assure Pharaoh that he and his family would return. In quoting his father's words (Gen. 50:5), Joseph was careful not to mention that Jacob specifically requested not to be buried in Egypt (47:29–30).

—*Be Authentic*, page 179

4. What is significant about Pharaoh's decision to honor Jacob in death? What does this say about the value of honoring others' traditions? Pharaoh didn't have to do anything nice for Jacob or any of Joseph's family, yet he was very generous. How is this an example of God blessing His people in creative ways?

## From Today's World

The Bible records many stories of burials. In nearly every case, the descriptions suggest elaborate or at least well-thought-out ceremonies and mourning that went on longer than a few hours. Today, with the instant access to information, news of a person's death can travel at the speed of emails and text messages. While this means those who care for someone who has passed can learn of the passing more quickly, it also means that the news isn't always treated with great reverence. A Facebook status update or email might be the only way someone hears about the passing of a friend.

5. How has the information age affected the grieving process? What are the benefits of the Old Testament approach to grieving the loss of a loved one? How can we maintain the best aspects of that sort of mourning today? How do we show reverence in death when the news of it is often relegated to a few characters typed on a computer?

## From the Commentary

When death invades a family, and you've done all you can to honor the deceased and comfort the sorrowing, there comes a time when you have to return to life with its duties. This doesn't mean we forget the deceased, but it does mean that we put our grief into perspective and get back to the business of living. After all, the best way to honor the dead is to take care of the living. Prolonged mourning may bring us more sympathy, but it won't develop more maturity or make us more useful to others.

—*Be Authentic*, page 180

6. Review Genesis 50:15–21. What did Joseph and his family do after mourning the death of Jacob? How do you know when the mourning period is over?

## From the Commentary

After all that Joseph had done to encourage them, it was cruel of his brothers to say, "Joseph will perhaps hate us and pay us back for what we did to him." (We often suspect in others what we'd do ourselves if we had the opportunity!) When you doubt God's Word, you soon begin to question God's love, and then you give up all hope for the future, because faith, hope, and love go together. But it all begins with faith: "So then faith comes by hearing, and hearing by the word of God" (Rom. 10:17 NKJV).

What the men should have done was to sit down and calmly review all that Joseph had said to them and done for them. In many tangible ways, Joseph had demonstrated his love and forgiveness and had given them every reason to believe that their past sins were over and forgotten. They really had nothing to fear.

How do we know God loves us and forgives those who put their faith in Christ? *His unchanging Word tells us so.* "These things I have written to you who believe in the name of the Son of God, that you may know that you have eternal life" (1 John 5:13 NKJV). How we feel and what God says are two different things, and we must never judge God's eternal Word by our transient emotions. "Who shall separate us from the love of Christ?" asked Paul, and then he proceeded to answer the question: *Nothing* (Rom. 8:35, 38–39).

—*Be Authentic*, pages 181–82

7. Why did Joseph's brothers still think he was going to pay them back for what they did to him, despite all the evidence to the contrary? Why do people so quickly move from believing to mistrusting? Where do you see that same kind of skepticism in today's world? How can trusting God help us to trust one another?

## From the Commentary

Joseph must have summoned his brothers to his home, for it's not likely they would go there on their own. When they arrived, they fell prostrate before him in fear, their last bow in fulfillment of Joseph's prophetic dreams. Like the Prodigal Son, they couldn't accept free forgiveness. That was expecting too much! The brothers offered to become servants and work their way to the place where Joseph could forgive them and accept them (Luke 15:19). If that's your approach to forgiveness, read Ephesians 2:8–9 and claim it.

The only people God can forgive are those who know they're sinners, who admit it and confess that they can't do anything to merit or earn God's forgiveness. Whether it's the woman at the well (John 4), the tax collector in the tree (Luke 19:1–10), or the thief on the cross (23:39–43), all sinners have to admit their guilt, abandon their proud efforts to earn salvation, and throw themselves on the mercy of the Lord.

Joseph didn't minimize their sins, for he said, "You intended to harm me" (Gen. 50:20 NIV). He knew that there had been evil in their hearts, but he also knew that God had overruled their evil deeds to accomplish His good purposes. This reminds us of what happened on the cross. Peter said, "Him [Jesus], being delivered by the determined purpose and foreknowledge of God, you have taken by lawless hands, have crucified, and put to death; whom God raised up" (Acts 2:23–24 NKJV). Out of the greatest sin ever committed by humankind, God brought the greatest blessing that ever came to humankind.

Joseph not only forgave his brothers, but he also assured them of his constant care. "I will nourish you, and your little ones" (Gen. 50:21). He gave them homes to live in, work to do, food to eat, and provision for their needs. Once again, we see here a picture of our Savior, who promises never to leave us or forsake us (Matt. 28:20; John 6:37; 10:27–29; Heb. 13:5–6) and to meet our every need (Rom. 8:32; Phil. 4:19).

—*Be Authentic*, pages 183–84

8. How does God assure His children that He has indeed forgiven them and forgotten their sins? (See Isa. 12:2.) Why might some Christians think it's a mark of humility to be fearful and insecure about their salvation? How is this actually evidence of unbelief?

*More to Consider: How can each of the following Scripture passages assure us about forgiveness: Micah 7:19; Isaiah 38:17; 43:25; 44:22; Hebrews 8:12; 10:17; Colossians 2:13; 3:1–11?*

*From the Commentary*

Whether you look at Joseph as a son, a brother, or an administrator, he was certainly an exceptional man. Because of Joseph, many lives were saved during the famine, including his own family, and therefore the future of the people of Israel was guaranteed. If the family of Jacob had died out, the world would have been deprived of the Word of God and the Son of God. So we owe a lot to Joseph.

Joseph was seventeen years old when he was taken to Egypt (Gen. 37:2), and he lived there ninety-three years, fifty-one of them with his beloved family near him. During those years, he saw to it that the Jewish people were cared for and protected, for God had a special work for them to do. He became a grandfather and then a great-grandfather!

"By faith Joseph, when he was dying, made mention of the departure of the children of Israel, and gave instructions concerning his bones" (Heb. 11:22 NKJV). God's promises to Abraham (Gen. 15:13–16) were passed along to Isaac and Jacob, and Jacob shared them with Joseph (48:21). Faith isn't a shallow emotion that we work up by ourselves, or an optimistic "hope-so" attitude of "faith in faith." True faith is grounded on the infallible Word of God, and because God said it, we believe it and act upon it.

—*Be Authentic*, pages 185–86

9. Review Genesis 50:22–26 and Hebrews 11:22. In what ways does true faith lead to obedient action (James 2:14–26)? How was Joseph's life an example of true faith? What does the fact that he maintained his faith apart from his family and in a foreign land teach us about the persistence of faith? About Joseph's relationship with God?

## From the Commentary

According to Hebrews 11:13–16, the patriarchs confessed that they were "strangers and pilgrims on the earth." A vagabond has no home; a fugitive is running from home; a stranger is away from home; but a pilgrim is heading home. They had their eyes on the future, the glorious city that God was preparing for them, and they passed that heavenly vision along to their descendants.

Living like a pilgrim isn't a matter of geography but of attitude: You feel like a traveler and not a settler. You tend to feel temporary, wondering if you really belong here and your eyes have that faraway look.

Pilgrims make progress. If you stand still in your life of faith, you've ceased to be a pilgrim. There are always new promises to claim, new enemies to fight, and new territories to gain. Pilgrims have many privileges, but one privilege they don't have is that of standing still and taking it easy.

—*Be Authentic*, page 196

10. What are some of the ways the patriarchs in Genesis lived as pilgrims? What were some of the great accomplishments God gave them? What roles did they play in God's divine purpose? How are we today like pilgrims? What are some of the ways God is using us in His divine plan?

## Looking Inward

Take a moment to reflect on all that you've explored thus far in this study of Genesis 50. Review your notes and answers and think about how each of these things matters in your life today.

*Tips for Small Groups: To get the most out of this section, form pairs or trios and have group members take turns answering these questions. Be honest and as open as you can in this discussion, but most of all, be encouraging and supportive of others. Be sensitive to those who are going through particularly difficult times and don't press for people to speak if they're uncomfortable doing so.*

11. What is your experience with mourning? If you've lost a loved one, how did you process your grief? Did you spend enough time in mourning? Too much? What role did your faith play in the grieving process?

12. Have you ever experienced something similar to Joseph—when his brothers suddenly distrusted him after the death of their father? What are the triggers that make you suddenly stop trusting what someone is saying?

13. Do you feel like a pilgrim? Why or why not? What are some of the ways you are progressing in your pilgrimage of faith? What are some roadblocks you've faced along the way? How can you trust God when you run into roadblocks in the future?

## Going Forward

14. Think of one or two things that you have learned that you'd like to work on in the coming week. Remember that this is all about quality, not quantity. It's better to work on one specific area of life and do it well than to work on many and do poorly (or to be so overwhelmed that you simply don't try).

Do you want to learn how to mourn the loss of loved ones in a way that honors God? Be specific. Go back through Genesis 50 and put a star next to the phrase or verse that is most encouraging to you. Consider memorizing this verse.

> *Real-Life Application Ideas: Think about the pilgrim journey that you're on. What are some of the markers along the journey so far that illustrate progress? Note these in a journal, then make a commitment to add to the journal as you continue along your path of faith. To add some extra dimension to your journal, read the book* The Pilgrim's Progress *by John Bunyan and jot down some of your thoughts about the book as well.*

## Seeking Help

15. Write a prayer below (or simply pray one in silence), inviting God to work on your mind and heart in those areas you've noted in the Going Forward section. Be honest about your desires and fears.

*Notes for Small Groups:*

- *Look for ways to put into practice the things you wrote in the Going Forward section. Talk with other group members about your ideas and commit to being accountable to one another.*

- *During the coming week, ask the Holy Spirit to continue to reveal truth to you from what you've read and studied.*

# Summary and Review

*Notes for Small Groups: This session is a summary and review of this book. Because of that, it is shorter than the previous lessons. If you are using this in a small-group setting, consider combining this lesson with a time of fellowship or a shared meal.*

*Before you begin ...*
- *Pray for the Holy Spirit to reveal truth and wisdom as you go through this lesson.*
- *Briefly review the notes you made in the previous sessions. You will refer back to previous sections throughout this bonus lesson.*

## Looking Back

1. Over the past eight lessons, you've examined Genesis 25—50. What expectations did you bring to this study? In what ways were those expectations met?

2. What is the most significant personal discovery you've made from this study?

3. What surprised you most about Genesis 25—50? What, if anything, troubled you?

## Progress Report

4. Take a few moments to review the Going Forward sections of the previous lessons. How would you rate your progress for each of the things you chose to work on? What adjustments, if any, do you need to make to continue on the path toward spiritual maturity?

ɔ. In what ways have you grown closer to Christ during this study? Take a moment to celebrate those things. Then think of areas where you feel you still need to grow and note those here. Make plans to revisit this study in a few weeks to review your growing faith.

## Things to Pray About

6. Genesis 25—50 focuses on the theme of authenticity. As you reflect on the various characters and how they did or didn't live authentic lives, consider how they might inspire you to make wise choices in your own journey.

7. The messages in Genesis 25—50 include trusting God, the importance of family, living with integrity, mourning loss, and following God's lead even when it seems difficult. Spend time praying for each of these topics.

8. Whether you've been studying this in a small group or on your own, there are many other Christians working through the very same issues you discovered when examining these chapters in Genesis. Take time to pray for them, that God would reveal truth, that the Holy Spirit would guide you, and that each person might grow in spiritual maturity according to God's will.

## A Blessing of Encouragement

Studying the Bible is one of the best ways to learn how to be more like Christ. Thanks for taking this step. In closing, let this blessing precede you and follow you into the next week while you continue to marinate in God's Word:

*May God light your path to greater understanding as you review the truths found in Genesis 25—50 and consider how they can help you grow closer to Christ.*